TRAILBLAZER FOUNDERS

"Deepti Pahwa has recognized that successful entrepreneurship is, fundamentally, about prospective entrepreneurs acquiring the power to turn their dreams into reality. That holds also for the women and minorities historically so vastly underrepresented in the start-up world. With inspirational stories of founders with underrepresented backgrounds, Pahwa seeks to inspire others—many others—to follow in their paths."

— JEFFREY PFEFFER, THOMAS D. DEE II
PROFESSOR OF ORGANIZATIONAL BEHAVIOR AT
STANFORD'S GRADUATE SCHOOL OF BUSINESS
AND AUTHOR OF 7 RULES OF POWER.

I have always taught that few principles are more important for entrepreneurs to keep in mind than "people do business with people", a point that Deepti repeatedly emphasizes in this highly practical and easy to read book. In Trailblazer Founders, Deepti illustrates that in order to build great businesses you need to start with building meaningful relationships — with investors as much as with those who join your enterprise. And to build those relationships much more broadly than you might initially believe is necessary. Unfortunately, this is an aspect of success that many entrepreneurs tend to overlook and a skillset many don't realize can be learned and leveraged. I recommend this book to anyone who is looking to think outside the box of how we have traditionally thought about venture and entrepreneurship.

— CAROLE ROBIN, PH.D. AUTHOR OF CONNECT:
BUILDING EXCEPTIONAL RELATIONSHIPS

"The remarkable "Trailblazer Founders" is a celebration of success that showcases the incredible determination, creativity, and persistence of successful entrepreneurs and leaders, who despite all challenges paved the way for the next generation to do better. Brimming with evidence-based strategies, this powerful guidebook reveals how to create your own captivating personal brand, acquire influence, and persuade stakeholders through strategic networking, and build a village of support around your startup idea. Make no mistake: "owning your power" is the key to success and this book will equip founders with the resources they need to blaze their own trails. An absolute must-have for any aspiring entrepreneur, this book will ignite the fire within you and set you on a course for greatness."

"Trailblazer Founders by Deepti Pahwa provides Founders a roadmap to navigate the complex and confusing entrepreneurial ecosystem."

— RAHUL BHANDARI, FOUNDING PARTNER AND ADVISOR, REACTION (GLOBAL SUSTAINABILITY FUND)

Deepti presents a collage of stories and insights from prominent VCs and successful entrepreneurs in an easy-to-read fashion. Entrepreneurs will be inspired and learn how to navigate the challenges of entrepreneurship to chart their paths to success.

— RADHIKA IYENGAR AND JORDEN WOODS, FOUNDING PARTNERS, STARCHAIN VENTURES

Trailblazer Founders is a collection of valuable lessons and timely stories from several diverse founders who have successfully reinvented themselves and created their own ladder in order to make a huge impact. Infused with hard-won wisdom, this brilliant book serves as a practical toolkit for aspiring and early-stage founders who could use a jolt of inspiration and an insightful roadmap to grow and scale their ventures by leveraging their influence.

— SALEEMA VELLANI, FOUNDER & CEO OF RIPPLE IMPACT | AWARD-WINNING AUTHOR OF INNOVATION STARTS WITH I

"Deepti is a phenomenal innovation coach, and her book is a must-read."

"Deepti has created a strong innovation community for founders within Stanford University Ecosystem to collaborate, share ideas, and learn from each other. This has enabled innovators to pursue their passions, overcome challenges, and make a positive impact. The world is better because of her!"

"This book might hold the mindset-shift that changes your future. With honest curiosity, Deepti Pahwa explores the secrets of unlikely founders—the ones who have succeeded despite having the deck stacked against them—to find lessons for the rest of us. We idolize too many founders who started with a big check from their parents. Deepti has devoted herself to discovering how to build a company when your only natural advantage is your own drive. For years, the only people fortunate enough to learn from her have been those who got into her

accelerator, or who worked with her. This book is a can't-miss opportunity to see what has worked for entrepreneurs who had to do it on their own."

— ROBIN COLEMAN, FOUNDER,
WRITELIKEANEXPERT.COM

Having co-founded the Stanford LEAD Incubator and Startup Accelerator (LISA) with Deepti, it is an honour to work with her and to call her my friend. In Trailblazer Founders, Deepti shares her vast knowledge and experience with the world. This is a must read for all new and serial entrepreneurs. You will quickly learn why countless startups from around the world rely on Deepti's mentorship and value her opinion so highly. Like the reader, I am constantly inspired by Deepti's expertise and vision.

— EDWARD MUNDT, LISA CO-FOUNDER;
SENIOR GLOBAL TREASURY CONSULTANT

"A refreshingly candid, informed, and tactical playbook for all trailblazer Founders in the making. Deepti Pahwa provides compelling truths, often beyond conventional wisdom, making clear her mission to empower an entirely new generation of visionaries."

— PHILLIP MOHABIR, CO-FOUNDER
& CEO VIVO SURGERY

"A fascinating and well-researched book that will change the way you think about innovation and entrepreneurship. This book provides a unique perspective on leadership, along with practical steps and tools to help readers on their own journey."

— ALINA ADAMS, FOUNDER & CEO, ARTVEOLI, INC., SOCIAL ENTREPRENEURS MENTOR - MILLER CENTRE FOR SOCIAL ENTREPRENEURSHIP, SANTA CLARA UNIVERSITY

"This is the pep talk every aspiring entrepreneur needs in order to confidently charge ahead. Deepti's book is full of direct advice from VCs and entrepreneurs sharing surprisingly simple yet profoundly important ingredients for success, all delivered through an engaging storytelling style that makes this a must-read page turner."

— THERESA M. LINA, SILICON VALLEY BUSINESS STRATEGIST AND AUTHOR, BE THE GO-TO

"Deepti is taking on a bold task in this book - to challenge the reader that their limits are imaginary, that anyone can break through the invisible wall, shake off the imposter syndrome, and deliver a vision of the future that can make the world a better place. Equal access to opportunity is not a given in the world we live in today. Through practical advice, Deepti walks us through ways to level the playing field and elevate

founders into success for a more equitable world, no matter the starting point."

— ROMAN ARCEA, PRODUCT MANAGEMENT AT GOOGLE, ACCOMPLISHED PRODUCT, ENGINEERING AND CONSULTING LEADER AND MENTOR

There are so many books about VCs and founders, but this one takes on a truly novel perspective by letting the founders tell their own stories. Deepti's ability to emphasize and analyze their context and motivations makes this a top choice for Entrepreneurs, including anyone working with startups.

— ASGER TRIER BING, SERIAL ENTREPRENEUR – IMPACT

"Trailblazer Founders is the ultimate guide to transforming yourself from dreamer to doer. With real-life experiences, social and behavioral science strategies, Deepti Pahwa unlocks the power skills needed to break through invisible barriers and achieve greatness. Join the movement of determined and resilient entrepreneurs who refuse to let gender, race, or cultural background hold them back. Let Trailblazer Founders

inspire and empower you to take action, overcome obstacles, and become the unstoppable protagonist of your own story."

— HELIO MOSQUIM JUNIOR, TECHNOLOGY EXECUTIVE, VALE. MATCH4ACTION CO-FOUNDER WITH CROWDDOING FOR SYSTEMIC CHANGE

"This book of stories of trailblazer founders is a masterclass in the power of storytelling to change the world. Deepti Pahwa, herself a trailblazer, with her own inspiring story, has shone the spotlight onto the most inspiring people who have made their difference their superpower. This book tells us more about those who have turned the obstacles put in their way into even greater value through courage, determination, and unstoppable energy. They have fought through fear, doubt, and blockages to shine even brighter. The book converts these stories into clear steps for your own entrepreneurial journey. If everything is harder for you, know that this makes your story even more valuable, and even more crucial that you embrace it. This book tells you how to leverage your story so you too can make a unique impact on the world. "

— EMILIE WHITE, FOUNDER & CEO - PAPER PLANES

"I want to give "Trailblazer Founders" to everyone wanting to engage, inspire and get sponsors at different levels of the organisation - not only to entrepreneurs. In the end, we all have ideas to sell in the corporate world - not only internally

but also externally to get trust, commitment and move our ideas or projects forward. *Deepti Pahwa has shared a goldmine of insights - it makes you feel galvanised and energized with every page.*"

"Trailblazer Founders" is an incredibly inspiring piece of literature that every aspiring entrepreneur should possess. It highlights the exceptional bravery, ingenuity, and tenacity of those who have paved the way for us, motivating us to aim for greater accomplishments. The book is a rare gem that brilliantly combines gripping anecdotes with astute counsel, making it the most exceptional and invaluable resource I have encountered in quite some time."

"Deepti Pahwa leverages her executive coaching experience and expands her impact by presenting Trailblazer Founders, a book in which Pahwa suggests how to successfully develop your startup and get from zero-to-one from a social science point of view. The exposed strategies do normally require the deliberate exposure to uncomfortable social situations, but these are exactly needed to succeed! It explains stories collected from founders that also belong to minority groups – unfortunately

heavily underrepresented in the startup world – giving any founder (or founder-to-be) the chance of perform a critical reflection and obtain the necessary power to be successful."

— ERIK MOLINA NILSEN, MANAGING DIRECTOR (MD) AT TRIFORK SPAIN, A NASDAQ CSE LISTED COMPANY

"Polish Executive Presence - No one is going to invest in your Imposter Syndrome' - Deepti Pahwa's book Trailblazer Founder is a bold & honest sketch of the what and the how for your journey to a Trailblazer founder. With a collection of powerful stories, she leaves the reader with actionable insights that truly can be life-changing."

— MADHAVI RAJAN, DIRECTOR OF BUSINESS ACCELERATION, CSO OFFICE, INTEL CORPORATION

"The remarkable "Trailblazer Founders" is a game changer book for successful entrepreneurs and leaders. This book distills complex concepts into clear and actionable advice. It's a must-read for anyone looking to succeed in the competitive world of business, and I'm confident it will become a staple on the bookshelves of entrepreneurs and business leaders everywhere. Pahwa has drawn on her own experiences and provided real-world examples, making the book not only informative, but also engaging and enjoyable to read: A valuable resource to

the business community, and for inspiring the next generation of leaders to achieve their goals."

"Comprehensive entrepreneurship advise from a Founder to other Founders... from someone who is right there working on the link between innovative ideas and impactful & successul enterprises!"

"Trailblazer Founders" is a must-read. Deepti Pahwa helps you navigate every step of your journey with her invaluable insights and experience, coupled with inspiring stories from founders and seasoned VCs worldwide, showcasing how diversity can be a source of power in realizing success. Whether you are just beginning your journey as an entrepreneur or already have years of experience in the field, this book will provide the guidance and motivation needed to take your business to the next level. «Trailblazer Founders» is an inspiring call to action

that encourages entrepreneurs to be the protagonists of their own stories—highly recommended!"

"Deepti Pahwa reveals the secrets of successful entrepreneurs that we would fail to spot in plain sight. It is not about the ideas, but the people who (re)present them: How do they behave? What do they do to inspire the confidence of investors, partners, clients? Trailblazer Founders contains precious practical advice, a guidebook for founders, startups, and all who aspire to a career or business growth. Take notes!"

"Deepti Pahwa nailed it. Peppered with inspiring stories and anecdotes, the Trailblazer Founders offers the Power framework for influence and stickiness that every entrepreneur should master."

"If you are not yet out of your comfort zone, Deepti gives you a path to challenge yourself. "Trailblazer Founders" will boost your self-confidence and guide you through your start-up journey."

— VALERIE ANDREY, FOUNDER AND
CEO OF VAS BEYOND CX

"Through Deepti's extensive knowledge and experience woven together with real-life observations and interviews, this book provides a step-by-step guide for founders to get ahead of the game. That being said, despite not being a founder myself, I was drawn in from the very beginning reading the opening paragraph. This book is a must-have source of inspiration for anyone in business!"

— FUMI MEYER FUJITA, EC EXPERIENCE MANAGER

"Trailblazer Founders is an essential read for any aspiring entrepreneur. Through her insightful stories and empowering advice, Deepti lifts up the veil of obscurity and guides readers to success with the development of valuable skills and knowledge that can help anyone from any background turn their ambitions into a reality. This book isn't just a guide to success, it's a manifesto for all dreamers to realize their

potential, challenge boundaries, and take their business to the highest heights."

— EVE VLEMINCX, STARTUP MENTOR
& EXECUTIVE COACH

TRAILBLAZER FOUNDERS

BREAKING THROUGH INVISIBLE BOUNDARIES

DEEPTI PAHWA

NEW DEGREE PRESS

TRAILBLAZER FOUNDERS
Breaking through Invisible Boundaries

ISBN   979-8-88926-908-3 *Paperback*
        979-8-88926-909-0 *Ebook*

For Mom and Dad

CONTENTS

"There are no limits to what you can accomplish, except the limits you place on your own thinking and actions."

BRIAN TRACY

INTRODUCTION

Falguni Nayar dared to defy all expectations when, at the ripe age of fifty, she set out to embark on a journey of transformation. With a revolutionary vision for beauty retail and an entrepreneurial force of nature, she initiated her start-up Nykaa. Despite the risks of disrupting traditional retailing, Falguni confidently founded Nykaa in 2012 with a goal to revolutionize the beauty industry (Singh 2021). From being privately held to going public in November 2021, Nykaa's shares skyrocketed 89 percent within twenty-four hours. The company was valued at a whopping $13 billion—establishing Nayar as an undisputed unicorn in India.

Armed with nothing but a vision and a few meager contacts, she plunged into the unknown and unforgiving world of entrepreneurialism in 2012. Technology was an ever-present barrier for four long and arduous years, threatening to strangle her fledgling venture in its infancy. All she had to lean on were her keen networking skills, undeterred will, and relationships built over her banking career. The combination helped unlock capital and other barriers; with it, she set out determined to defy the odds and prove her doubters wrong.

Sara Blakely had no background in fashion, retail, or business, yet she defied the odds and founded Spanx in 2000. After coming up with the idea to make her white pants look better, her fortune skyrocketed, and in 2012 she became the youngest self-made billionaire ever crowned by *Forbes*. Now, at fifty years of age, her fortune stands tall as a testament to her success—her net worth of $1.2 billion climbs higher after an incredible deal with private equity behemoth Blackstone (Makinson 2021).

After launching Spanx, Blakely set her sights on the highest peak of success. She knew she had to make a move with the big guns and sent a selection of her products to *The Oprah Winfrey Show*, knowing that was the only way to turn her dreams into reality. By being featured in "Oprah's Favorite Things," her brand skyrocketed, allowing her to achieve her lifelong goal of working on Spanx full-time. QVC was another giant platform that helped Blakely's shapewear to gain traction, more so when she appeared on Richard Branson's reality TV show, *The Rebel Billionaire*. Branson made a generous donation of $750,000 for the foundation of the Spanx by Sara Blakely Foundation.

Sara Blakely is a powerful example of an individual's initiative to pursue a "crazy dream," even when others don't believe in one's idea. She started her business out of her apartment, with $5,000 of her personal savings, and created an entire billion-dollar shapewear industry. She was determined to make her product a household name, cognizant of the importance of media in building her personal brand. Unafraid of the spotlight, she seized every opportunity to establish her presence. Her ambitious and confident approach to public exposure was a major factor in her incredible success.

Daymond John's meteoric rise to fame began long before he appeared as a judge on ABC's *Shark Tank*. If legend is true, his entrepreneurial spirit was present as early as first grade, when he sold customized pencils to his classmates.

John's true success began in 1992 with the launch of FUBU, his streetwear clothing company. Through an ingenious strategy of lending clothes to popular musicians and featuring them in music videos, the company quickly gained widespread recognition—and with that recognition came great success (Taylor 2022).

These founders stared into the unknown abyss of the future, their vision illuminated by a kaleidoscope of possibilities. They knew that others do not have the courage or imagination to envision the future they see so clearly. They have been the bearers of their story, projecting it to all those who wanted to join them in the adventure. The passion drove them to leave the world better than they found it, and they had the courage to muster the resources needed to make this dream come true.

Indeed, they also faced incredible odds as they gathered the strength and resources necessary to bring their vision to life. Although they were met with fear, doubt, and uncertainty along the way, they had the ambition and courage to push forward.

The tales of these daring entrepreneurs are the epitome of perseverance and courage. Nothing could stop them from achieving greatness. They had something special that set them apart from the rest, something that propelled them to these heights. Through their incredible tenacity, they smashed societal expectations and shattered the stereotype of the billionaire entrepreneur, boldly blazing a unique path to success.

These stories are the ultimate demonstration of principles, mentalities, and strategies coming to fruition that are laid out in this book. These founders disregarded any preconceived notions of what they were capable of and instead relied on their own qualities to bring them influence. They did this by building power, influencing the outcome, and manifesting their ideas into multi-dollar businesses.

TIME FOR A GREAT CORRECTION IN ENTREPRENEURSHIP AND VENTURE CAPITAL

The venture capital space remains largely male-dominated and inaccessible to many. Global VC assets hit $1.3 trillion under management in 2021, having had a huge impact on global economies, driving innovation and development. Yet, women remain underrepresented (Blee et al. 2021).

A December 2020 headline from *Crunchbase News* tells the story: "Global VC funding to female founders dropped dramatically this year." In the same time frame, global VC investments grew 15 percent year over year, to $259 billion, and US investments reached an all-time high of $130 billion, according to a PwC and CB Insights report. This is even worse when we look beyond just the gender lens and add the racial divide to it. A total of ten Black female entrepreneurs received venture capital investments (0.02 percent of the total amount invested) across the ten years, with none so far receiving late-stage funding (Teare 2020).

It also found just one early-stage (series A or B) venture capital investment recorded for a Black female, compared to 194 early-stage investments in white female entrepreneurs. Investments to Black founders account for less than 1 percent of all venture capital—and the number hasn't changed much in 2020. People have been reporting on these industry numbers for years.

In 2020, venture capital investors funneled $150 billion to start-ups. But only approximately 1 percent of those funds were distributed to Black founders. Despite the rapid growth of Black entrepreneurship, there is a vast—and growing—funding gap (Ross and Lounibos 2022).

As people become more aware of the importance of these issues and existing biases, we have seen more conversations about how to make institutions and venture capital firms more diverse. I fully endorse this effort. However, will government-backed proposals and venture investors committing to multicultural and gender diverse founders lead to fundamental change?

Unless we change narratives, bring forth powerful role models from all corners of society, and actively celebrate the achievements of a diverse group, our attempts at institutional reform will barely make a dent.

External societal barriers are not the only ones preventing founders to gain access to capital and networks. Internalizing the negative messages that society conveys creates further limitations. Indeed, investors need to become more diverse for change, but entrepreneurs must also recognize the revolution within. To create real progress, both sides must address the situation.

ORIENTING OUR IMAGINATION TOWARD THE OPPORTUNITY IN FRONT OF US

Celebrating the awe-inspiring stories of individuals who challenge the status quo defines our sense of what is possible in the present and future. The old guard is changing, as younger generations are not concerned with traditional biases and divisions. Therefore, instead of focusing on recounting and quantifying the historical "problem," let us orient our imagination, creative energy, and persevering spirit toward the opportunity.

I'm not sure one can emphasize this point enough. Opportunity is not limited by gender or ethnicity. It is a matter of understanding the entrepreneurial ecosystem and how to navigate within it. While different personalities will naturally have different perspectives, talents, and strengths—and, as such, differing leadership styles—there are, nonetheless, certain core attributes of successful leaders which can be acquired and deepened. In all cases, we must learn how to weave something out of nothing; how to build from "zero to one" and then "one to hundred and beyond."

THE INVISIBLE BOUNDARIES: THE FIRST OBSTACLE IN YOUR WAY IS YOU

The most daunting secret that most founders struggle with is the all-encompassing feeling of not belonging. No matter how anyone identifies themselves—in terms of cultural background, gender identity, beliefs, or age—imposter syndrome looms in, ready to swoop in and take control.

This book seeks to empower, educate, and transform so that we may create new realities through recounting the stories of bold pioneers and inspiring role models. These people are as real as it gets, having walked the path to success. These stories are meant not only to inform and inspire, but also demand a change in the current narratives. It is a call to ask ourselves: What stories are we telling ourselves? What stories are shaping our lives and communities?

At the end of the day, the only language investors and stakeholders understand is the hard currency of money.

They are seeking to maximize returns through the ruthless minimization of risk. That's the cold, hard, simple calculus. The same irresistible logic applies across industries, whether we're talking about movies, music, or start-ups. Those who control access to funding are searching desperately for a safe bet, a sure thing proven to succeed in the past. Everything else is just a gamble as they wait to find out what will be "hot" in the next moment.

For creative, innovative visionaries, this can be a frustrating (if not simply boring) reality to navigate. Still, the system isn't airtight. Occasionally, through sheer perseverance or cosmic luck, some indie effort sneaks through. Against all odds, after many failures and pivots, this "new possibility" somehow succeeds. And then everyone is chasing after the new trend, trying feverishly to replicate its wisdom and charm, but failing to realize it all comes down to the individuals and teams who bring their passionate ideas to life.

BREAKING THROUGH INVISIBLE BOUNDARIES

Again, we're talking about stories. Successful founders see into the future. They see what others cannot yet see, for want of imagination and vision. They see the end in the beginning. They are the only ones capable of communicating this story to would-be partners, investors, and employees alike. If they put their mind to it, they're able to marshal the financial and human resources in helping to leave the world a little better than they found it.

This is the crux of the matter, its big punchline. Despite anyone's inherent crisis of confidence, venture capitalists do not somehow hold the keys to launch our business. They are not the arbiters of all that is good and true. Investors do not have an uncanny ability to fathom the long-term viability of our enterprising vision. Oftentimes, in fact, it's quite the opposite. The story we've been telling ourselves—we have it backwards.

The truth is that we are the protagonists of our own story. We perceive that a successful outcome is not only possible but assured. Without entrepreneurs, investors are just sitting on a meaningless pile of cash. We are offering them an opportunity to leverage business as a force of good. Plenty of funds are available in the world. It's our unique challenge to find the right partners with whom to collaborate.

Inevitable difficulties and challenges are ahead. But with clarity of purpose, we can articulate the value proposition for our partners to rally their support. Slowly but surely, the historical inequities are being evaporated in the bright light of a new day. While replete with inspirational accounts of women and non-white founders, we are seeing a surge of stories that go beyond the categories of identity and ethnicity.

A NEW NARRATIVE

Eleanor Roosevelt once famously said: "No one can make you feel inferior without your consent." It would be an unfortunate self-narrative to assume that multicultural founders are somehow at a disadvantage in today's capital markets. All other things being equal—and equally considered—women and minorities automatically stand out among the multitudes who seek funding. I believe sincerely, in the depths of my heart and bones, that people want to invest in and lift historically underserved communities. The only real question is if investors can buy into the story of the founders and their teams to deliver exceptional returns.

Entrepreneurship is a skill set which anyone can learn, embrace, and leverage for positive outcomes. It's kind of like running a four-minute mile. It's incredibly challenging, but not impossible. Once you've seen that others have been able to do it, many more are suddenly following in their footsteps.

This book is for the ambitious and unyielding, the determined and resilient. It's for anyone with the drive to achieve greatness regardless of gender, race, or cultural background. It delves deep into social science and behavioral cues, arming you with the knowledge of what you can use to your advantage to overcome your biggest obstacle—yourself!

The key to unlock the potential of your entrepreneurial venture lies within you.

GROUNDBREAKING MOVEMENTS START IN UNEXPECTED PLACES

This book is a clarion call to action for founders to become the protagonists of their own story. Distilled from hard-won experience and dozens of interviews with trailblazer founders and seasoned venture capitalists, it provides a roadmap to navigate the entrepreneurial ecosystem. You will learn about leadership skills, research-based tools, and an actionable framework necessary to manifest your ideas into powerful strategies.

Put the principles and tactics into practice as you go along. Regardless of your background or circumstances, you can begin your journey to greatness once you gather the strength and self-confidence to step out of your comfort zone. Shifting behaviors is a quiet act of learning. If you wait until you master it to dive in, you will expend a great deal of energy. That is, if you ever get started.

THIS BOOK CAN HELP YOU:

- Understand the entrepreneurial ecosystem and acquire core attributes of successful founders.
- Utilize social science to acquire influence and persuade investors, stakeholders, and customers.
- Make bold moves—neutralize the founder stereotype.
- Take advantage of social capital to realize your entrepreneurial goals.

- Build a captivating personal brand that has investors competing to collaborate with you and stakeholders willingly sharing resources for you to grow.
- Increase your worth to your network, especially investors, communities, clients, and stakeholders.
- Build your village: Make your start-up idea stick with communities that helps build traction.
- Gain exposure and access to optimal opportunities.
- Develop a strong executive presence and overcome biases.
- Overcome imposter syndrome and internalized negative messages from society.

You will unlock the full potential of this book if your thirst for learning is only outdone by your desire to take action.

The Fourth Wall

She watched them from the darkness as they moved across the well-lit stage, words echoing off the invisible wall and into the audience. She had seen this play before, so many times, but she still felt enthralled, her eyes trained on the performers, drawn to the subtle nuances of their movements and the intensity of their speeches.

She marveled at the invisible barrier between stage and audience, the one that separated the watcher from the watched, the quiet observer from the passionate participants.

She ached to step foot on stage, but a force she could not understand or see stopped her. She longed to join in the performance, become an actor on the stage, but a part of her couldn't help but feel intimidated by this barrier; this fourth wall.[1]

Maybe if she just took one step forward and shouted out her lines with confidence, they would accept her into their world? Maybe if she just reached out and grabbed hold of someone's hand, they wouldn't push her away? She felt stuck in limbo between two worlds— one inside the fourth wall and one outside—and she wasn't sure how to bridge that gap.

---

1   The fourth wall is an invisible boundary between those delivering a performance and the people who are watching it. The phrase comes from the world of theater, where it represented the imaginary wall between the stage and the audience.

But then, as if on cue, her gaze suddenly shifted from the actors on stage to the audience behind her; those who had already managed to make it onto the other side. With newfound hope, she watched as they cheered and laughed at moments only they could see.

The fourth wall was supposed to be impenetrable—but clearly it wasn't!

She may not have known exactly how they'd done it yet, but at least now she knew it was possible; that maybe someday soon even she could find a way through and join those performers onstage!

SECTION 1

THE CONTEXT

CHAPTER 1

THE SMART MONEY: VC INSIDERS' TAKE ON THE "INVESTABLE JOCKEY"

"I'm a people investor—my job is to sit across the table every day and listen to some lunatic tell me about some future that I have never imagined, and try to figure out which lunatic I want to go on the adventure with."

RANDY KOMISAR, KLEINER PERKINS

"Raising venture capital is the easiest thing a start-up founder is ever going to do."

MARC ANDREESSEN

My gaze was immediately drawn to the wall behind David's desk, where an incredibly varied collection of artwork hung. A significant amount of thought and effort went into what he had curated there. He welcomed me with a warm smile and beamed as I inquired about the various pieces. His eyes seemed to come alive as he spoke, recounting his journey of acquiring each. A young woman's work depicting the Asian experience hung next to a dog painted by an eighty-five-year-old artist. The green painting was from Linus, who was going through gender-reaffirming surgery at art school when he painted that, and then there was Chantel Jofy, who completed her self-portraits after her divorce.

His enthusiasm was infectious as he pointed out other pieces on the wall—all created by diverse artists—and talked of their struggles, backgrounds, and triumphs. He continuously stressed the importance of these tales and described how he felt strongly connected to them. "This is Sasha Gordon, another young Asian painter who talks about being a heavy-set woman and feeling like the world isn't very kind to them." He continued, gesturing toward an artwork in the corner, discussing how it depicts Mexican immigrants. Seeing David's strong passion for these pieces, it was clear that stories speak deeply to him and that he values perspectives from different cultures. Each piece in his collection had been carefully chosen out of respect for empathy and inclusion.

David Hornik's insights on venture capital were invaluable to my book. With over two decades of experience in Silicon Valley, he is undeniably amongst the most influential and impactful people within the industry when it comes to understanding how venture capitalists choose to back a start-up.

David is a founding partner with Lobby Capital and the creator and executive producer of The Lobby Conference.

He invests broadly in information technology companies, focusing on enterprise applications and infrastructure software, fintech, and consumer-facing software and services. He is the author of the first venture capital blog, *VentureBlog*, and the first venture capital podcast, *VentureCast*. Before Lobby Capital, David was a general partner at August Capital for twenty years. He also teaches business and law at Harvard Law School and Stanford Graduate School of Business.

I asked him why he chose to be a part of my book. He leaned back in his chair, clasped his hands, and began to speak, "I get lots of emails daily. People reach out through various channels. And the reality is that my business is a people business. I know every great thing that has happened in my fifty-plus years of living has resulted from amazing people. And so, my natural inclination when people reach out with a question or a proposition is to say yes. Now, that's hard to fit that many yeses into any given week. But on the other hand, if it is particularly about sharing my general philosophical belief that can make a difference, I'm pleased to be part of that conversation."

The horse you choose to ride—what is your "why."

I asked, "Is there anything stronger than a great story?" David's eyes sparkled with recognition. His excitement seemed to grow with every narrative, as though reliving small triumphs gained over decades of working in Silicon Valley. Filled with anecdotes about audacious founders, take-charge pitches, and savvy "secret sauces," it felt more like a meeting between two fellows sharing tales rather than a book research encounter—one that left me suitably inspired and enlightened.

He was most passionate about how certain founders had managed to use their ability to tell a compelling story and had drawn him to their "why" to get his office door opened.

He enthusiastically shared, "Recently, I funded EarlyBird Education. It is doing early detection of dyslexia in children at a very young age. And I'm dyslexic and have had challenges." He swallowed hard, emotion still palpable in his voice. "The founder, Carla Small, told me about her son's struggles with dyslexia and the difficulties she faced trying to get a diagnosis in time. She created Early-Bird Education to help parents and children get the early help they need—and that resonated with me. I just had to help her."

Rather than looking at their ideas or the market opportunity, he is deeply interested in understanding founders and their motivation. He believes that understanding this "why" helps him comprehend their commitment and dedication, which makes all the difference in the long run. "So, I think there's not a single entrepreneur I fund where it doesn't start with—who are you, and why are you doing this? Or, what have you learned in your life that has led you to make this thing interesting?"

Through personal experience and his interactions with various ambitious entrepreneurs, he has heard countless examples pointing to their life stories' power. And story after story, his underlying message is clear: the "why" behind start-ups matter just as much as the ideas themselves.

Leaning forward in his chair, his hands on the table, he looked intently. His lips curled into a half smile, he said, "In fact, there's nothing I like less than a founder who tells me they are excited because they saw the biggest opportunity in the market or the best way to make money or did a market map to discover a missing piece. I don't find that a compelling story. Entrepreneurship is way too hard to be driven by some gray space in the market. That's not inspiring."

Swapna Gupta has a very similar outlook. She says, "The most underrated skill of a founder is the vision: Is it short term or long term?" Founders often think about the next one or two years, and they say all the right things in the pitch because that's what they have been trained through the community and network. But the more you peel, you realize how short-term or long-term they think. She said, "I go back to my assignments in equities and finance and look at founders from the perspective of: Are they thinking of it as a war or a single continuous series of matches to get to the end?"

As I met Swapna to discuss my book, the intensity in her eyes and the passion for the work she did stood out. As a Brown, bright young woman, she did not fit the stereotype of someone dominating the venture capital space. Her perspectives were essential to the narratives of this book. Her presence and impact in the industry are a powerful reminder that anyone can upset the status quo—an important motif throughout my book.

Swapna Gupta is a partner at Avaana Climate and Sustainability Fund, leading investments into technology-led start-ups catalyzing climate solutions and sustainability and delivering exponential returns. Before joining Avaana, Swapna led India investments at Qualcomm Ventures. She invested in various companies, including *Locus*, Shadowfax, Ninjacart, Zuddl, MoveInSync, Reverie, and Stellapps.

Swapna also launched Qualcomm Women Entrepreneurs India Network (QWEIN), a first-of-its-kind networking, learning, and mentoring program for deep-tech, early-stage female entrepreneurs in India. Swapna's stellar work in the ecosystem is recognized worldwide. She was also recently recognized by GCV as one of the top fifty emerging leaders in the corporate venture community and was the only one from India on the list.

AND WHY YOU?

I sat in front of my laptop, staring into the eyes of a man in his mid-forties. He wore a plain black T-shirt and conservative glasses. In his thick British accent, reflecting on his childhood, he remarked, "I have a very conventional and slightly boring upbringing, and that led me to do a

quite conventional and boring career, at least initially."
He added, "So, I was a corporate lawyer doing private
equity and M&A (mergers and acquisitions) for almost a
decade, working with a US firm while based in London,
predominantly, but it's been a little bit of time in Silicon
Valley, and then I moved to another law firm briefly until
I finally escaped. Today, I am a venture capitalist."

Chris Smith had quite a few stories to tell. He had seen
both sides of the start-up world: thriving and struggling.
With an entrepreneurial spirit and investor know-how, he
knew what it takes to create success. He joined Playfair
Capital's second fund as a VC in 2018.

He spoke passionately, his words punctuated by emphatic
gestures with his hands. "A founder needs to be able to
tell a powerful story. But it's more than just having an
interesting tale. It's about having the right combination
of traits that inspire us to believe they are the ones to
build this company."

He gives the example of Liz Gilligan of Material Evolu-
tion. Liz did the Techstars program run in conjunction
with The Heritage Group. She was introduced to him by
a member of his Kauffman Fellows class. He leaned forward on the edge of his seat, a spark of enthusiasm in
his voice. "I can't imagine there are many people in the
world as obsessed with cement as Liz. On our first call,
I remember the incredible scale of the problem—cement
causes 8 percent of global CO_2 emissions—and immediately believing that Liz was the person to solve it." He
adds, "Why? Expertise (a PhD in cement) and energy in

equal measure. It is so rare to meet a scientist who is also personable and can sell. "

In my conversation with David, he also shared a similar opinion. His voice was enthusiastic as he recounted his twenty-three-year collaboration with entrepreneur René Lacerte. David explained that René had grown up helping his parents and uncle with payroll and had an intimate knowledge of the industry's needs. When he shared his idea for PayCycle with David, René's passion for making payroll easier for small businesses was evident. David added, "He went on to establish PayCycle, which quickly became successful enough for him to sell to Intuit. Later, René started Bill.com, taking inspiration from how he lived among small business owners and knew how hard it is to manage the money in a small business."

David said, "René always had a unique perspective and experience in each venture. He spoke of starting businesses tailored to the deep problem he was trying to solve, and it was clear he understood the nuances better than anyone else." He sat back in his chair and smiled, a glint in his eye. "You see," he said, "the story of your unique position, perspective, and experience to solve a problem always matters."

THE DETERMINED ENTREPRENEUR: PERSEVERANCE AND EXCEPTIONAL PERFORMANCE

Swapna talks about how persistence is essential to founder success and sheds light on how that can be judged before they fund an investment. "Persistence can be seen in your recent interactions. For example, we were looking to invest in a company. We shied away right before signing the term sheet because feedback came through our sources that the person doesn't stick to the problem statement."

She emphasizes how important it is for a founder to stick to their guns. "The problem at a start-up is a problem-statement to be solved that could take several years. Do you have it in you to continue to get there? Over time, it may become boring." She discussed how she has seen founders where, at some point while building a company, things become very operational and less creative. "Do you have it in you to continue to stick around for the boring and mundane? And sometimes they hide their lack of determination by saying, 'We are second-time entrepreneurs.'" She paused as she smiled. "Well, that excuse does not work, because we all can go to the past jobs and the past lives of the founder to get the information we need."

When talking about the grit and endurance of founders, David recalled, "There is one founder in particular whose story is astonishing, and when you hear it, you're stunned at his capacity to shine, despite a lot of quite unlikely circumstances. And that's a gentleman by the name of

Wences Casares." His voice rose with intensity. "So, in my first meeting with Wences, we just talked about him, didn't even begin to get to his business."

Wences is an Argentinian entrepreneur based in Silicon Valley. He is an extraordinarily successful entrepreneur who built the most prominent digital bank in South America in the early days of the internet. "His story is about growing up on a ranch without reliable electricity, without reliable access to education, and the challenges he went through to ensure he got an education. Then, he had the challenge of building a company with his mother's little money she had saved up. So, it's just an astonishing story of grit, intellect, effort, and ultimately incredible triumph."

At Playfair Capital, they look at perseverance from the lens of exceptional performance, specifically for first-time founders. Chris illustrates this point by explaining how they filter founders, even before they look at a deck or the LinkedIn profile. "We're looking for some evidence of exceptional performance. And we think about that in the broadest possible way, largely because we back mostly first-time founders."

He gestured with his hands for emphasis as he explained how they judge the potential of a start-up founder. "To the point about women founders or underrepresented founders—it's often more difficult for them to prove exceptional performance through the traditional means." He added, "So if exceptional performance in the past was like, they did XYZ at Goldman, or they were at Microsoft or Google—we think about it far more broadly." He raised his eyebrows and nodded as if to say he would give those people a chance.

He proudly recounted the success of their portfolio founders, describing George Richardson of AeroCloud as a "professional racing driver" who'd been part of the Ferrari team for three years. "George talked me through his experience, which included being on the podium at Le Mans with the Ferrari team and driving at the Nurburgring. It struck me that somebody who could live on the edge racing supercars would be perfectly positioned to manage the ups and downs of entrepreneurship and to build a start-up. "

He added, "It demonstrates that no matter what your background, if you have excelled at something, you have many of the core attributes of a successful entrepreneur—perseverance, commitment, and working under intense pressure. You don't need an MBA and a few years' experiences in the 'right' company to become a successful start-up founder." But to Chris' point, it is just as essential to communicate your story as it is to have a story!

He added another example of Conor Sheridan, who had built a fast-food fried chicken business in Dublin before founding software company Nory. Raising his eyebrows, Chris added with admiration that both George and Conor had "exceptional performance" in the past. He elaborated, "There's a mixture of exceptional performance and founder-market fit. And we value exceptional performance because we can judge that if this person is likely to do well under pressure, they're likely to have perseverance and have all these sorts of fundamental character traits that make a founder investible."

He explained that one way to judge a founder's resilience is to look for any challenges they may have faced. Being an entrepreneur is always challenging, and even the most successful companies have had times where they almost failed. He mentioned, "And so, actually, someone who's had a very linear experience, perhaps been in the comfort of a corporate environment all the time—it's something that we dig into a little bit deeper. We'd like to see that perseverance where they stayed on course where things have been a little more difficult."

"But, eventually, what is important to us," added Chris, "is what we call sustainable persistence, meaning they will keep pushing and driving the business, but sustainably in that they recognize the need to find time to rest, to recuperate and not burn out. Sometimes, in the first two to three years of building a company, we have founders who don't take a single day vacation, and often we're talking to them saying you have to look after yourself. You have to find a balance and move at an incredible pace. Building a start-up is a marathon, not a sprint!" The best founders know when to take a break.

There is no such thing as a lazy entrepreneur—"knowing the knowable."

David adjusts himself on his chair as he speaks. "I often talk about this idea that I'm interested in funding experts. But the problem is that people often confuse that with having a PhD or working in an industry for twenty years. And those things could be great. My firm funded a brilliant professor at Stanford. She was convinced that RF technology had reached the point where data could travel through the air. And so she was the expert in inventing Wi-Fi, which she did! And that's an easy story to tell."

David sat up, enthusiastic as he illustrated another example. "But on the other hand, I funded these two young guys who were out of college—one had started law school, and the other one had maybe started in a bank. But they had never established expertise in anything specific," he said. "But they became focused on the broader payments ecosystem, on what it would take to allow people to pay and manage shared bills. That's when they created WePay."

"Even though they were not experts in payments or money movements, their enthusiasm and creativity garnered excellent answers for every question I asked." David smiled. "They were just obsessed with solving a tough problem." He quickly noted that "it's not enough to be creative. You need to thoroughly understand how systems work today, why things you do work well, and where there are opportunities to change the things that exist. Only then will creativity be helpful." It's clear from David's example that these two truly hustled and achieved something extraordinary without any expertise in this area.

"You have to do all of the work to understand everything that is knowable," he emphasized, his voice resounding with conviction. "Why? Because the challenge with entrepreneurship lies in that which cannot be known beforehand. Simply put, you ought to know the knowable stuff. It's table stakes. And then, to succeed," he continued forcefully, "great entrepreneurs leverage their experiences and contexts, tap into their creativity and intellect, while also fostering relationships. These enable them to get through those moments of unknowability."

Chris shares the same outlook as David. He adjusted his glasses as he equated this quality of founders who try to grasp everything knowable with an analogy. "They're like sponges for information," he said. "They learn at a remarkable rate and never become complacent or think they know it all. All they want to do is continue learning and having the best people around them in the form of mentors, advisors, or investors. In a funding round, for instance, they'll prioritize investors who can provide guidance over the best valuation."

BUILDING A BRAND AND CREDIBILITY

David reflects on the importance of being visible by shedding light on his own example. "I became a venture capitalist when I had no business being a venture capitalist. Before becoming a VC, I had been an attorney for six years, starting as a litigator and then as a corporate and licensing attorney. I then suddenly became a venture capitalist."

"To be a successful investor, I had to hear about people's stories. And to do that, I had to let people know I'm a venture capitalist." And so even though no one was blogging about venture capital at the time, and the venture industry was very isolated, he thought, *Wouldn't it be better if entrepreneurs knew what venture capitalists thought? Wouldn't it be better if someone who would present to me understood why I cared about their financials?*

David saw the value in having a blog dedicated to venture capitalism and was the first to make a move. He created *VentureBlog* not necessarily for his benefit but with the understanding that entrepreneurs could appreciate what he was offering. Starting the blog ended up being an incredibly smart decision, because it gave him visibility in the public space, which suddenly humanized him and made him more accessible. People started to notice who David Hornik was and why they should trust him as a venture capitalist. Then, the conversation changed from "Who is David Hornik?" to "Have you read what David Hornik thinks?"

He equates this example to how founders could similarly gain credibility and be visible by carving out their space through thought leadership. He elaborates, "There are lots of ways to establish credibility, many ways to get known, and many ways to be heard. And, by the way, one of the things that I have always done and is a critical long-term strategy is to be helpful to others."

He mentions that he often has founders who talk about him, saying, "Although he didn't fund my company, he introduced me to someone, or he gave me some advice that helped me rethink how I would go to market, etc." He impressed that if you are helpful to people (and not because you're trying to get something in exchange), over a long time, people recognize that you want to create positive change in the broader ecosystem, and they want to help you do that.

The power of your story lies in its ability to be heard and to reverberate and penetrate the hearts and minds of an audience. As such, it is essential to ensure your story is effectively communicated and given the appropriate platform, media, and vehicle to reach its intended listeners. It also involves actively seeking out the necessary channels and networks to grant you credibility and reach.

Chris's career as an investor is no small feat. His powerful entrepreneurial spirit has enabled two wildly successful business adventures. He never shies away from publicizing the firm's ventures in press releases and blog posts.

As Chris says, and David concurs, "Seeing is believing," They preach what they practice: be bold, be visible, and get noticed.

In 2007, Chris made his second trip to Silicon Valley while working with a law firm. His curiosity was piqued. He began to explore the tech ecosystem, venture capital, and angel investing. When he returned to London, he shifted his focus to building a parallel career that was just as fulfilling. He dove into angel investing zealously, funding fifteen start-ups over ten years. As he talked about the founders and their stories of determination, it was a creative outlet for him. His investments eventually paid off, with six companies experiencing exits, a few going public, and four being acquired. His accomplishments had filled him with pride. It was a not-bad track record.

He spoke with passion and confidence as he recounted his entrepreneurial experiences. "I felt like I was onto something with investing. Before joining Playfair Capital, I moved to the Isle of Man and worked for a B2B (business to business) telecoms business, Planned.com. There, I had the challenge of building a team from a small set of eight to nearly one hundred people in five years. We grew the business from nothing to nearly $60 million in revenue. It was an amazing opportunity that taught me so much."

He ran his hand through his hair and leaned back, revealing more about his current role at Playfair Capital. "I was putting together a blog post yesterday, and I was shocked. I was adding up all the rounds our companies have done this year. Almost half a billion dollars have been raised by our companies—which blew my mind." He laughed, shaking his head. "I just still can't quite wrap my head around it, given the size of our fund, which is $32 million." He stretched his arms out wide and began to pace. "And 30 percent of our founders are women (cofounders or founders), compared to the industry average, which is more like 10 percent."

He stopped abruptly and leaned forward, his eyes intent. "This was a very long introduction to say how we think about founders we invest in."

He underlines the importance of building a team: "The biggest piece of storytelling and networking isn't about getting investors. It's about hiring the right people with your story." He explains that having great talent in your early stages can set you apart from your rivals and make you a successful company. He adds, "You need to convince people to work for you since they will take risks. You most likely haven't raised money yet at this stage, and your brand is unknown. Therefore, your ability to tell your story and make people enthusiastic is essential." He highlights the importance of leveraging media, blogging, and press coverage to garner the attention of talent and venture capitalists for subsequent funding rounds.

Swapna talks about why there's a reason second-time founders charge a premium, as they've created that brand of someone who has successfully built and exited and returned the money to their shareholders. She says, "If you're a first-time founder, and if you're building something in hydrogen space, for instance, and for the last ten years you become an evangelist or leader in that space, chances are I will speak to you to understand what you're doing." Therefore, personal brand matters in hiring and getting advisors, allowing you to raise continuous capital.

She adds a commonly known example to explain how critical brand building is: "I do feel Elon Musk does whatever he does to win capital every day of his life, and he's building cash-guzzling businesses. If he is not in the public eye for 'good, bad, ugly,' I don't think he'd be able to raise the kind of capital he does." She highlights the point we will discuss in one of the chapters later: As a founder, you must constantly build a brand that attracts people, especially in businesses where you need capital.

SHOW UP WITH CONFIDENCE AND OWN UP TO YOUR SUCCESSES

Swapna's face lit up as I asked her about any differences in cultural or gendered attitudes she might have observed among the start-up founders. She nodded enthusiastically, eager to share her favorite example. "I remember this woman who came in to pitch with her cofounder. During their introduction, she spoke for only twenty seconds, while her male counterpart spoke for a full minute and thirty seconds. Clearly, she was the 'heavy lifter' of the two—she had spearheaded the idea and the start-up—yet she gave him the floor to talk."

David thinks there's much speculation and conversation on the topic, but the evidence to back any of it still evolves. David furrowed his brow as he thought about his recent encounters with minority founders. He said, "There's certainly a sense when I talk to female entrepreneurs that they are often more apologetic about things that have happened in the past. On the contrary, men are quick to claim successes they haven't had, or about claiming expertise they don't possess."

Another thing David saw in his personal experiences: "When men are in an organization that is successful, they are very quick to claim credit. When women are in an organization that is successful, they are very quick to explain what small role they played in it."

He paused, letting his words sink in. "I think there's a difference between men and women in this regard."

He added, "I'd much rather know what you did. And, therefore, you have more credibility." In entrepreneurship, a lot of it is about convincing people to do challenging and unlikely things. "The more confidence you project, the more you can express the belief you're the right person to get funded, the more likely you will hire the right people to manage your company, the more likely you will convince clients to adopt your solution."

FOUNDER TO CEO: SECRET SUPERPOWER THAT INVESTORS VALUE!

Swapna leaned back in her chair, an expression of wisdom on her face as she elaborated on this skill with the ability to delegate. "Many founders don't understand the importance of delegation," she began. "It's like a plane that you're flying. You need to ensure that if something happens to you, someone else will be capable of taking the wheel and continuing your vision." She paused for emphasis. "Delegation and finding people more capable than you are essential to make your idea grow."

Swapna and Chris agreed that scaling is an essential part of success for a start-up, and that's where delegation comes in. Chris said, "To scale, these founders must become effective delegators. We are comfortable investing in them because we know they will figure out that the job of a CEO is very dry—business strategy, fundraising, and hiring." He adds, "Most of them are excellent at sales, for example. So what they need to do is offload all the other stuff."

"They're very good at seeing an org-chart in their head, delegating and offloading tasks. Most importantly, they're also confident in hiring people who are better than them. There's no ego at all. They want to hire people who are smart, who are hungry, and who can continue taking work off them." Chris believes that delegation piece is key, but not often talked about.

TYPES OF INVESTORS AND THEIR INVESTMENT PREFERENCES

If you're looking to raise capital for your start-up, it's essential to understand which type of investors might be the most beneficial.

Angel and venture capital (VC) funds are the two main types of investors in the market. Angels are typically high-net-worth individuals who can fund companies in exchange for equity or convertible notes.

To qualify as an angel investor, individuals generally need an earned income exceeding $200,000 annually or a net worth exceeding $1 million. VC funds, on the other hand, are entities that invest in start-ups professionally and require more traction than angels for investment. For pre-product or pre-revenue start-ups, angels may be the ideal option; however, if you have some revenue and growth to show off, then VC funds and angels are both viable options. Angel investors boast high levels of market knowledge, expertise, and invaluable contacts, which can propel a venture from its humble beginnings to incredible success.

You must also understand their investment thesis, from the industries they prefer to the verticals they specialize in and the business models they support. With this knowledge, you can pinpoint investors who finance in your specific market and can add tangible value to your start-up. Think of sectors like DeepAI, healthcare, fintech, and SaaS. Understanding the industries that appeal to potential investors will help you narrow down and secure the right partners.

You can't afford to ignore what kind of investments stage a VC makes. Failure to do so will be a waste of time. Pre-seed, seed, series A, and higher—they have their segment that they would invest in. Pre-Seed is for emerging companies that have no revenue or product yet. If you're looking for investments here, angels are your best bet. Money flows freely into companies in the seed stages—venture capitalists and angels stake a claim. Series A funding and more are for the ventures that have developed their product or market fit to perfection. If you have made it so far and your product shows enough promise, the sharks are circling with their pocketbooks open wide.

Last but not least, geography looms large in the investment landscape, with investors preferring to keep their portfolio founders closer home. Even within nations, the geographical divide can be stark. Investors from the East Coast, for example, may loathe traveling to meet with their portfolio start-ups on the West Coast in the US. The TechCrunch article, "Where and why venture capitalists invest close to home," cites the reason for this: "There's a positive, self-strengthening cycle of growth and reinvestment as successful entrepreneurs become investors with a vested interest in fueling the next cycle(s) of growth in their respective communities" (Rowley 2017).

THE HUMAN FACTOR

Venture capitalists may be driven solely by financial gain, but there is much more to their decisions than meets the eye. At their core, venture capitalists are people, and connecting with the business and entrepreneur personally can be incredibly powerful in swaying their investment. You can forge deep connections that stir emotions and make the VC passionate about the project, inspiring them to commit.

People buy from people—nowhere is that more applicable than when you're seeking capital to grow your business. To attract investors, it is essential to creating meaningful relationships that showcase more than just data points. The human factor is invaluable when networking your venture and should never be overlooked. Investors need to be convinced of both the tangible opportunity to make money and the intangible trustworthiness of their partnership. The values and goals shared must align with those of the potential funder. Impress that they can trust in you and that you will deliver far beyond their expectations!

FIND YOUR EDGE AS AN INVESTABLE JOCKEY:

1. Identify and communicate your "why" instead of focusing on the biggest gaps in the market that would make money.
2. Communicate why you are uniquely positioned to build your venture.
3. Know the knowable.
4. Invest in a brand and credibility to build visibility.
5. As first-time founders, reflect on what you have done in the past that could qualify as "exceptional performance."
6. Showcase your expertise, knowledge, and proficiency in dealing with people.
7. Show up with confidence and own up to your successes.
8. Ensure your communication is clear and consistent, so your message is preserved.
9. Research different types of investors to find a fit before reaching out.
10. Remember: People buy from people. Nowhere is that more applicable than when you're seeking capital.

Above all, let your passion shine through. Captivate investors with your enthusiasm for the project or business opportunity, and show you have something even more precious than money behind it.

CHAPTER 2

THE JOCKEY VS. THE HORSE: WHAT COMPELS THE INVESTMENT DECISION

At the heart of this new economy are two essential elements: ideas and money. Venture capitalists, like master chefs in a kitchen, know how to source out the best of these two ingredients and mix them to yield success—without overlooking the right proportion.

Ensuring focus from the hordes of start-ups eager to achieve unicorn status and bring massive public offerings into their equation is critical. They must assess each start-up's innovative idea and determine if it is worth the financial investment required to push the venture through development. It can be a tricky task due to all the competition out there. They must measure how much they should invest in a company and when to generate value and take advantage of high growth cycles to maximize returns. Venture investors often follow a portfolio approach, investing in multiple companies with the expectation that many may fail. And only a few will scale and deliver significant returns to cover losses.

THE ODDS ARE ONE IN ONE THOUSAND

VC firms have their sights set firmly on sky-high returns, so their advice is tailored to those who are not content with mere success but are driven by an ambition to dominate the world. These companies must demonstrate they are unstoppable juggernauts. Most of their difficulties these companies will experience is proving to the VCs their goals will be significant enough to justify an investment.

Jeffrey Bussgang describes in his book, *Mastering the VC Game*, the venture capital investment process with hundreds of potential deals is a complex game of pattern recognition and guesswork. The VCs are on the hunt, searching for that one deal that gives them an unfair edge in their investments. Why you? Why now? On average, they comb through three hundred to five hundred ideas yearly and are only willing to gamble on one or two.

Once you get their attention in the early stages of evaluation, success is about turning your deal champion into an advocate, a salesperson who will introduce your idea to the rest of the VC partners. Only then can you hope to get the attention your business deserves (Bussgang 2011).

David nodded his head, his forehead creased in thought. "I get around a thousand applications a year, executive summaries and introductions included." He cupped his hand over his mouth as he continued. "Out of those, I'll probably take the time to have a few conversations with about a hundred of them. A meaningful conversation with about ten. And then one or two of those I'll introduce to my partners for further review."

He continued, "You should know that it would make no sense if you come to me to raise $100 million for your business, because that's not what I do. I don't invest in late-stage companies." Starting point for a founder should be making the right choice for venture capitalists or angel investors. Different investors finance at various stages of a business and make very industry-specific investments. Again, researching on what type of investor best suits your start-up needs is very critical.

He adds, "If you look at my history, you can know what I do. It's not confusing. Ninety-nine percent of the companies I fund are software companies. None of the companies I funded had been in the medical or biotech space. So, if you're a biotech founder and reach out to me, you're wasting your time and my time." He repeatedly emphasizes the importance of researching before reaching out to VCs. "If you want to know what people are interested in, look at what they've done in the past. People don't change on a dime. And when they do, they're explicit about it."

He refers to an example of his friend, Josh Belzer, who used to be an angel investor and invested broadly in good ideas. Then, he raised a new fund called Climactic to finance climate-focused start-ups. David added, "So now, if you go to him just because, in the past, he's funded social media, he wouldn't be interested as he has clearly stated on his website and publicly announced what he is interested in."

David grins. "Do the work to find out who is excited about the things you're building. You might get a chance at a conversation."

Chris Smith nodded in agreement. "Founders need to understand what we are looking for, the business we're in, and what we need to succeed." Most founders do not empathize and try to understand that VCs need considerable, billion-dollar-plus outcomes because they might only get one such start-up per fund, which drives the moderate majority of their returns. He adds, "We probably dismiss more than 50 percent of people approaching us with that pitch deck because their ambition is not big enough or the market size doesn't support the company we need to build. So understanding the business size you can build is almost like the first gating item."

He further expounded on Playfair Capital's approach to making investments. His hands gestured as he said, "We only make six investments a year, which is pretty contrary given that most early-stage VC funds want to do thirty to fifty checks and get some diversification and try and index the market."

He looked away for a moment, a distant gleam in his eye. "We also go super deep in diligence. We write forty-page investment memos. We apply almost like a series A level of rigor to pre-seed rounds. And I guess what that looks like to date is that of the companies we'd invest in, about 70 percent of those have gone on to raise series A. That's kind of our North Star metric of how many companies we can convert to series A."

THE INVESTOR DEBATE: THE HORSE VERSUS THE JOCKEY

There is often a debate on the more robust indicator of start-up success—the founder or the idea. Who gets invested in: the jockey (start-up founders) or the horse (great ideas with potential)? Who better to answer this question than the venture capitalists themselves? Although, usually, they have a hard time deciding what matters the most.

Dan Matthies and I have known each other for two years as part of the Stanford Alumni Association. We've frequently shared insights into the burgeoning world of entrepreneurship and venture capitalism. He has been an invaluable part of some of the initiatives I lead, for instance, judging a couple of times with LISA, the incubator I cofounded at Stanford GSB LEAD.

Whenever I've engaged with Dan, I've been impressed by his intellect, curiosity, and never-ending quest for knowledge. He's always kept his finger on the pulse of the hottest, most promising start-ups. His optimism is balanced by an exceptional ability to deconstruct an idea, ferreting out any weaknesses in the business model, technology, or regulatory compliance. He pushes for perfection out of a genuine desire to see his investments succeed.

As we got on the video call to discuss my book, he sat tall, broad-shouldered, wearing a classic shirt and collars tucked in his polo. His deep voice had an East Coast accent, echoing his charismatic smile. Behind him was a stark black backdrop set with the company's logo in white, providing a striking contrast. He then referred to Ilya Strebulaev's research: "What VCs invest on depends a bit on the stage. If it's early stages, then you're investing in the jockey. You have to believe in the person to create the horse. For later stages, take Microsoft or Amazon, for example—even though Bill Gates has left, it's still a great horse with a new jockey leading it." He smiled and concluded, "You're betting on Microsoft."

He finished his thought and said, "The early-stage venture capitalists usually take a more hands-on approach with their investments and so invest in founders," he said. "But once a start-up has demonstrated the ability to grow revenue and capture market share, the relationship dynamics might change. It could even become necessary to bring in new leadership, or a 'jockey,' because the founder was a sprint jockey. And now you need somebody who will be the scale jockey."

Dan Matthies is a proven business builder, operator, and leader of global businesses. He is the founding general partner of Reaction. With over fifteen years of experience building and managing global tech businesses, Dan has demonstrated an unparalleled knack for seeing the big picture. A brilliant alum of Stanford University, the Wharton School of Business (MBA), and The College of New Jersey (Finance and International Business), Dan is a trailblazer in the VC and entrepreneurship space.

Dan leaned back in his chair and placed his hands on the back of his head, deep in thought. He pondered the horse versus jockey debate further. "In healthcare and pharmaceuticals," he began, "the horse is more important than the jockey because of the science. Without an aha moment or a breakthrough, no matter how incredible the leader or founder is, there's nothing to invest in or sell."

He offers further insights on jockeys, those who "kill the horse" because of their lack of clarity, focus, and ability to execute. He adds, "So many founders are naive and just want to do everything for everyone instead of having a clear focus. And they might be great technical founders or science founders. But their ability to execute or bring in someone to execute isn't proven, so you wonder, is this going to be another great idea that dies in the lab?"

He illustrates this with an example: "We met with a company called Rebellyous Foods in Seattle last week. And this woman founder is working on alternative meat space. I'm not sure if you know that there are thirteen hundred brands other than Impossible Foods and Beyond Meat."

He emphasized, "There are thirteen hundred brands that have the same strategy: to have the best science, the tastiest alternative meat, and drive that into a new brand."

Dan vividly remembered the conversation with the Rebellyous Foods founder. She stood before them, her eyes piercing and stern as she spoke. "It won't work," she said. "People care about price at the end of the day. And lowering the price premium now in this industry can kill it because things are so expensive. If you put a premium on a premium product, you'll price yourself out of the market."

He added, "So, she narrowed down her strategy. Over five years, she has proven that she can execute on building the tools to be able to build high quality, high scale, low-cost alternative chicken patties nugget strips. To continue to move those KPIs (key performance indicators), now she's at parity and selling millions of dollars' worth of this chicken and has the scale up to become the powerhouse for plant-based chicken. She has the technology to serve other brands with manufacturing-as-a-service, which no one else has."

He marveled at her business acumen, clarity of thought, and ability to hone in on the project that promised the most potential for profits. "Chicken," he said. "That's as much consumed as all the other meats combined. She focused on mainstream, price parity, and a clear solution to build, clarity on having a team to build the technology, and getting the customers interested in going down that path, and hence a soon-to-be profitable company."

Swapna sat silently, processing the question about jockey versus horse. Her eyes illuminated as she began to speak. "I always ask what kind of vision the founder has." She gestured with her hands, emphasizing her points. "First and foremost, you must be able to sell your idea and convince others it's worth investing in." She paused to let this settle in before continuing, "A great product is great, but I'm looking for a great salesperson who can articulate his vision to investors, teams, and partners. You might get the idea from zero to one if it is very compelling, but one to ten and ten to one hundred—all these journeys look very different." She concludes, "As a founder, I think you're always selling."

David Hornik discussed how the problem or its solution might sometimes only be known once someone comes forward with a bold vision. To illustrate his point, he talked about one of his investments—Splunk. "I had three smart founders who said wouldn't it be great if you could build a search engine that sat on top of log files." Splunk was working on the idea that having infinite amounts of data and the capacity to understand it would allow you to solve all sorts of big and interesting problems. Little did he know, the idea would revolutionize big data and lead to a multi-billion-dollar business.

David said excitedly, "I did not think about this problem or the solution before funding Splunk. I funded Splunk because the founders had a very compelling vision for how you could take data and make sense of it. It turned out that was not only a good idea but a very lucrative one." He said there could be hundreds of other such ideas with the power to change the world, but it takes someone passionate and committed to making it happen. The idea must reach venture capitalists with a compelling vision and strategy to solve the problem. "I won't know it until someone smarter than I tells me about it. Venture capitalists help amazing people solve problems." That's why venture capitalists exist—to help talented people make their dreams come true.

THE RESEARCH: JOCKEYS TRUMP HORSES IN RACE TO SECURE VC FUNDING

I posed a single question to each of my interviewees in this book—"The horse or the jockey: Which would you invest in?" Over and over again, I heard from innovators, VCs, accelerators, and other key players in the industry: The right team can make or break an idea and determine success. It is all about the leader—their strength, bravery, and charisma—that will draw together an unbeatable management team.

Hoping to uncover evidence that could support these opinions, I learned more about Ilya's research, which delves into the subject with intricate detail.

The "How Do Venture Capitalists Make Decisions?" report aims to clarify this issue. They surveyed 885 venture capitalists at 681 firms to uncover what drives their decision-making. It turns out it takes far more than a flip of a coin. On average, VCs evaluate and investigate nearly two hundred businesses a year but only choose one to invest in out of four. No wonder the VC evaluation process takes on average 118 hours of paperwork and research to make the right choice! This includes extended due diligence, such as asking ten different references for feedback to get a true feel of the company they are looking into. Thus, venture capitalists must ensure the criteria they use will lead them to a final four that gives the most significant long-term returns (Gompers et al. 2016).

Ilya Strebulaev, a Stanford Graduate School of Business professor of private equity, discussed his research in the article "Jockeys Trump Horses in Race to Secure VC Funding" (Strebulaev 2016). His research implies that VCs contemplate the management team, or the jockey, as the most influential factor.

"Jockey was rated most frequently not only as *'an'* important factor (by 95 percent of VCs) but also as *'the most'* important factor (47 percent of VC). Business- (or horse-) related factors were also rated high—business model, product, market, the industry—as the most important factor in investment decision-making by only 37 percent of VCs." He continues, "The situation gets more complex when accounting for VCs' investment stage or sector preferences. The team is more likely to be the most important factor for early-stage investors and investors in the IT sector" (Strebulaev 2016).

The report further found the results look different for later-stage investors or those who target the healthcare sector. This was the only subset in the study *not* to overwhelmingly identify a start-up's team as the most critical factor, giving priority to business models and company valuations (Strebulaev 2016).

The research suggests there is often an inflection point where the jockey fades into the shadows while the horse commands the limelight.

Ilya further sheds light on which individual characteristics of those founders' VCs consider most likely to contribute to long-term success. "Given that jockey, or people, factors are the most important drivers of investment selection, ability was—perhaps unsurprisingly—the most-mentioned factor. Experience in the specific industry was second, followed by passion, specific entrepreneurial experience, and teamwork."

There is nuance and variation, with healthcare bucking the overall trend. VCs targeting this space identified industry experience as the essential quality in a founder team. Passion was substantially less important. Meanwhile, California-based VCs appear to value passion more and are less concerned with experience.

Ilya's studies are consistent with earlier research on "Attracting Early Stage Investors: Evidence from a Randomized Field Experiment" (Bernstein, Arthur, and Kevin 2014). Broadly speaking, the jockey is highly important.

Ilya adds, "Founder teams doing the rounds in pursuit of investment—especially those at an early stage, or in the IT sector—could give their chances a considerable boost by emphasizing their personal capabilities, passion, experience, and relationships" (Strebulaev, 2016).

DO YOU HAVE IT IN YOU TO INSTILL THAT CONFIDENCE?

Start-up companies are often ambitious projects that require a significant amount of capital to get off the ground. Despite having great promise, most of these businesses make little to no money in the early going. It can be compared to betting on a newborn horse that may only reach its true potential if it is guided and trained by the right people and ridden by the right jockeys.

In horse races, the jockey may get the credit for the win, but the horse and the jockey are equally important. The same goes for start-ups. The idea provides urgency and motivation. It is the company's foundation. However, a start-up is only as good as its founder, who must have the necessary control, direction, and tactics to make it succeed. Even if a start-up looks excellent in theory, does its founder have what it takes to make it a success?

The history of entrepreneurship is littered with countless cases of unfathomable success achieved by an exceptional entrepreneur taking a good idea and converting it into a runaway success. Far fewer are the cases where a mediocre entrepreneur has managed to turn a great idea into a stellar success.

With the immense competition vying for venture capital attention, you must understand the power dynamics and how to play the game well. Those who want to stand out from the pack must possess a unique combination of idea, drive, intellect, connectedness in the investment community, a personal brand, confidence, and ten-fold the ambition.

When all these elements come together nicely, founders stand a better chance of impressing potential investors—knowing how to orchestrate wins in the boardroom while remaining true to themselves.

SECTION 2

THE MINDSET

CHAPTER 3

POWER AND INFLUENCE: BUILD IT BEFORE YOU NEED IT

"When you're talking to me in the first minute, I'm thinking—is this person a leader?"

—RON CONWAY, SILICON VALLEY
VC AND "SUPER ANGEL"

"The two fundamental dimensions that distinguish people who rise to great heights and accomplish amazing things are will, the drive to take on big challenges, and skill, the capabilities required to turn ambition into accomplishment."

—JEFFREY PFEFFER, POWER: WHY SOME
PEOPLE HAVE IT AND OTHERS DON'T

As Tristan Walker stepped on the stage, all eyes were on him. He was tall and stout with a next-door personality, yet it was evident he had done some remarkable things in his life. Although recognizable, his relaxed outfit of a gray sweatshirt, jeans, and white sneakers suggested he felt right at home in the spotlight.

He looked at the room full of Stanford MBAs from where he stood and said, "This view is way more intimidating!" (James 2023). The wooden background, with its prominent strips and Stanford Business School flags, gave an air of resilience to the atmosphere. After all, many powerful people had been in this same spot before him, telling their stories of success.

This person who was once amongst this audience had become the first Black CEO in the 180-year history of Procter & Gamble. He had drawn the courage to reach there from the same surroundings years earlier. Upon reaching the gray couch at the center stage, he poured himself a glass of water, ready to answer the questions. The atmosphere in the auditorium seemed electric with anticipation for what was about to unfold. It was clear this would be an insightful and captivating fireside chat.

"My life has been really about movement work, only doing the things that adhere to my values." Before starting his company, he had been working at Foursquare and Twitter. "Now, looking in hindsight, of course, Twitter was the place to work. But it was not that obvious back then when it had just started!" He continued, "Especially in the Stanford GSB context, many business school classmates chase sameness—the same jobs for the same roles! Little do we realize that sameness creates conflict, because you are chasing these finite resources, and that conflict leads to violence. And I think, for me, the thing that stood out was my difference."

Tristan Walker, Stanford GSB MBA, is the founder and CEO of Walker & Company Brands. He also serves on the Foot Locker and Shake Shack board of directors. *Fortune* magazine named him one of fifty of the "World's Greatest Leaders." In 2018, Tristan made a bold move, merging his brand with Procter & Gamble and becoming the first Black CEO under the P&G umbrella in the company's 180-year history. The Bevel brand was launched from this affiliation and widely distributed through the Target network.

Tristan saw an opportunity to become a voice for the African American community in the health and beauty markets. He knew from personal experience that certain products were often better suited to people of color, yet many felt underserved by standard products. Therefore, in 2013 he founded Walker & Company to provide tailored health and beauty products meeting this need.

His devoted Twitter following helped spread the word even more by offering a platform where he could get his ideas out there and make them accessible. He said in a deep voice, "Many entrepreneurs come to my office and ask me for advice to start a company and on raising capital. And I always ask a question in return: You want to start a company, but do you want to run it? And no one has ever had an answer to that question immediately" (James 2023).

"Ninety percent of my job is just people stuff. I do not focus on any product anymore." He added, "Being a CEO sucks. It is the worst job I have ever had. However, I cannot see myself doing anything else." Tristan shared lessons from the most challenging and rewarding years of his career.

"I realized I was a victim of bad circumstances and that I had something in me to create good circumstances, a lot of which I learned from here at Stanford." Tristan stands as an inspiring, modern-day example of a founder. He challenged the status quo with humble roots and a marginalized identity, showed success was possible regardless of background, and acquired an innate drive toward excellence and progress. He used many of the principles of building power and influence that we have yet to talk about in the context of entrepreneurship.

Today's more complex entrepreneurship terminology—phrases like "value proposition" and "product-market fit"—can obscure what it has always been about. Even the most incredible, revolutionary, game-changing idea will not guarantee success.

Contrary to popular belief, successful entrepreneurs are not always at the vanguard of coming up with groundbreaking ideas. While every invention is a major source of pride, having an exciting idea is not enough, and it is what you do that makes all the difference in whether your wildest dreams can become a reality. Most of the time, rather than reinventing the wheel, attaining success can be a matter of creating new or leveraging existing ideas;

focusing on what you are uniquely capable of creating; or more importantly, creating a market for that idea (brand building) and unlocking right resources to make the idea reach the world (like the right relationships with partners, investors, and influencers).

Larry Ellison is an incredible example of an entrepreneur's success story. His journey began when he created Oracle Corporation from nothing and eventually grew it into a multi-billion-dollar enterprise thanks to his unyielding work ethic and innovative leadership style. He carefully recruited top experts in the field and gave them the power to develop unimpeded. This combination of dynamism, determination, and creativity, and most importantly, delegating and empowering the teams to execute while he focused on the vision led to Oracle's success and becoming a leader in its sector.

Larry focused on the big picture and building relationships with influential people. He did not play by anyone's rules but his own. He is the longest-running founder CEO the tech industry has ever seen. Ben Horowitz of Andreessen Horowitz says that founder-CEOs are better than professional CEOs partly because they are committed to the company's long-term success. He also adds, "Being CEO requires a tremendous amount of skill. The larger the company becomes, the more skill that's required. We rarely meet a founder who has these skills at the time they found the company" (Horowitz 2010).

Entrepreneurship is often romanticized as a solo journey to riches, but the reality is that building a successful business is no small feat. For many entrepreneurs, the path to success is fraught with obstacles that do not always come in the form of a technical challenge. Achieving the dreams of a business requires more than simply building it. A strong leader must take charge. Acquiring the first talent to join the cause, building and managing a team smarter than yourself; managing board members; sailing through cofounder conflicts; and convincing the board of the strength of your vision for the company as it pivots and grows are some of the most challenging tasks an entrepreneur must face. Passion and persistence will be granted to you, but to be seen as an "investable" founder, investing in the right skills and mentality to influence the product's outcomes, must be a priority. Moreover, if you wish to keep your power to control your company's vision as it grows, you must start building that power now.

However, what is power, exactly? And how can you tell when you have it? Power is a complex and often misunderstood concept, especially in business. Power is your ability to influence an outcome. It can be found in many forms, from financial power to social power to positional power. The key is knowing how to identify and use the different types to achieve your goals.

For example, to secure the much-needed funding for your start-up, you must bring your A-game. You want to be well-networked to be reaching investors in the first place. And if you do not have the introductions through contacts known to them, your credibility, charm, and confidence would have to be on full display to establish a connection and build trust with the potential investor. You must dazzle them with the successes you have achieved while mitigating any potential risks. You must arm yourself with reliable data and a strong argument, then make your case for why investing in your start-up is wise. At the same time, you must connect with the investors emotionally and prove that you are the one for the job. Falling short in any of these areas will mean walking away empty-handed. Furthermore, if you reach a stage where you are on the other side of the table to negotiate a term sheet for the investment, you may find yourself subject to their merciless wheeling and dealings.

Alternatively, suppose you are negotiating with a supplier for more favorable terms. In that case, you may need to use your ability to unlock value in complex business deals and networking abilities to get what you want. You need to craft the vision you seek to project to build the confidence of your vendors, counterparts, colleagues, and the broader community. Similarly, when growing or managing your team, you must be able to motivate and inspire them to achieve common goals. This requires a delicate balance of maintaining authority while remaining open to input and feedback. If you come across as too autocratic, your team will become demotivated and uninspired. However, your team will become chaotic and unproductive if you are seen as too relaxed or laissez-faire.

Power is always a complex and nuanced topic for entrepreneurs. It takes ambition, courage, and foresight to understand the various forms power can take and to use them at the right time. With the right resources and frame of mind, you can shape the power around you and make it a force of success. Power appears in various manifestations, from the will to take on significant challenges to the capability to turn ambition into accomplishment while also enabling resources that enable you to embrace your opportunities and play your cards right.

WHY DO I NEED "POWER" AS AN ENTREPRENEUR?

In a podcast interview, "Psychology of Power and Influence," Deborah Gruenfeld, Stanford Graduate School of Business professor of organizational behavior, discusses her research. She talks about how "entrepreneurs are constantly faced with questions of power as they manage their growing teams, pitch to investors, and negotiate crucial deals for their growth. Even if they do not use the term power or think about power explicitly, it is something that is influencing them daily" (Teeter 2022).

She adds, "There is a mysterious force that can determine your success as a leader and an entrepreneur. I am talking about power" (Teeter 2022). She talks about how often start-up founders go from being a technology geek in a hoodie to someone who has hundreds of millions of dollars invested in them.

She argued how in a matter of days, these individuals need to learn how to show up in a way that conveys authority and power and makes others feel secure. It does not come naturally, and that is the challenge. This is because, on the inside, nothing feels different. They are the same person they have always been. However, to be successful as leaders and instill confidence in teams, people must learn how to put up those walls and show others they can take charge (Teeter 2022).

As an entrepreneur, you may start small with an idea and a few members on your team, but success leads to a more extensive operation of investors, a board of directors, and stakeholders. Going from a founder to a CEO can be daunting, as you must now answer to hundreds of employees and investors who have entrusted their livelihood and money in you.

Understanding the concept of power can help entrepreneurs make more strategic decisions about when and how to use their influence. Power is the ability to affect change. It can be personal power, which is internal and comes from within, or positional power, which comes from an individual's position within an organization. Personal power is often more challenging to quantify, while positional power is often easier to identify.

To lead the company successfully, CEOs need to learn not just operations strategies but also how to inspire, motivate, and command respect. This transformation requires impressive levels of poise, discipline, and confidence. They must learn how to get hundreds of millions of investment funds' attention and inspire those same investors with skillful leadership that extends beyond data or tangible returns. It is a challenging pivot full of professional and personal growth and can be intimidating. That is where power comes in, and learning how to acquire it becomes critical. Much of Gruenfeld's research is a good example, where she looked at how finding yourself in a powerful position is transformative in ways that often happen outside of our consciousness. We are often unaware we are being transformed by power (Teeter 2022).

UNDERSTANDING BIASES IS THE FIRST STEP TO BEATING THEM

After all, power is the ability to get things done. With a clear understanding of where it comes from, it can be easier to make progress. For many entrepreneurs, their power comes from their brand that can create opportunities that would otherwise be unavailable. It can also give them a platform to share ideas and build a following. Another source of power is their network, which provides access to resources, mentorship, and advice. Entrepreneurs themselves are also often a source of power. Their drive, determination, and willingness to take risks can inspire others to do the same.

But what do you do if, despite these skills and qualities, you are fighting against some implicit biases as a woman or minority founder? Understanding similarity bias and its impact on capital decision-making can be valuable in addressing what could be getting in the way of accessing the finance and necessary resources to back your idea and you as a founder.

When you walk into a room, what do you notice first? The shape of the room, the color of the walls, or the people in it? If you are like most, it is the latter. We are social creatures and naturally gravitate toward others we perceive as being like us. Now, visualize the group of friends you usually spend time with. Chances are they are close to the same age, gender, and cultural background as you. Despite our commitment to inclusivity and appreciating differences, we usually pick those with similar characteristics.

Forming relationships with people who have gone through the same experiences as you, like someone you play tennis with, or your friends from university, is natural. However, forming a preference for people similar to ourselves becomes problematic when it results in prejudiced behavior without us even realizing it.

This similarity bias takes shape in many forms, like establishing groups with similar values or interests. Inside these circles, those within the group often perceive one another as more skilled or talented than those outside it. This bias has been attributed to the large gender gap in venture capital investments, which has affected the entrepreneurial world. Investors disproportionately favor entrepreneurs with the same education, professional background, and experience as themselves.

The similar-to-me effect also adds the notion of stereotypes. We often assume that people from the same group will share the same personality traits as ourselves. We base this opinion on our prior knowledge and beliefs about what that group might be like.

Awareness of these biases and stereotypes and taking action to place yourself in positions where you stand to benefit from them can be a critical factor in breaking the bias and unlocking new opportunities. This really means finding commonalities with the group or people you want to approach. For example, as we saw in chapter one, David Hornik was compelled to help with the venture that solved for dyslexia in kids, as it resonated with his challenges with dyslexia. In other cases, it could also mean sharing similar hobbies, passions, or joining the similar clubs as the network you want to engage with.

FOUNDERS OF COLOR THAT CHANGED NARRATIVES

The narrative of founders from diverse backgrounds has evolved in recent years, with many individuals of color becoming successful entrepreneurs, venture capitalists, and leaders in the tech world. One brilliant example is Swapna Gupta, who I interviewed in this book. She mentions how she moved from a middle-class family having to even fight for her education to now being one of the acclaimed VCs in India.

She jokes candidly, "If I would not be doing this today, I would be perhaps making round Indian breads in some household." She constantly pushed the limits, stepped outside her comfort zone, and persevered until she achieved her goals. Her desire to make a difference led her to venture capitalism. As she described her journey, she noted, "I realized I could achieve two goals at once—investing and creating a positive impact."

She said, "As you look today, climate does seem to be the next big problem which needs solving. There are no climate funds in India. I found this great partner, Anjali Bansal, and we started this fund." Swapna mentions the importance of constantly getting out of her comfort zone to drive success: "A lot of my life has been driven by, *What can I do next?*"

Swapna gestured with her head as I asked her about the biases she may have encountered on her journey to becoming a venture capitalist. Her voice was determined as she declared, "I have read about those biases, but I have never felt them personally. If you are a younger person in the room, or you look different from the 95 percent of the rest, you have to work extra hard. But, once you have proven your legitimacy, it does not matter."

Her answer had the sentiment that echoed in all my conversations with founders whom I interviewed for this book. They were all immune to bias and believed they were no different. The barriers, the prejudices, the struggles never impacted their journeys.

David talks about one such trailblazer: "Tim Hsia is a young Asian man who went to Stanford from the military. He is someone whose identity is based on his service to the country. Ultimately, he decided to start a venture firm that invests in US veterans." He recalled, "Tim and I have been talking for now ten years. We first connected when I was teaching a class he was in. He asked me about the venture world, and I provided some guidance. My firm ended up interviewing him, and he started to think about launching a fund. Eventually, I became an official advisor to the fund he launched." He added, "He is not your typical entrepreneur, and he's not your typical venture capitalist."

He talks fondly of him and says, "You give him advice, and he listens. If there are three possible choices, he runs down all three. If he's having a consequential meeting, he reaches out to the people who will be most valuable in giving him advice in advance of that meeting and sets up a call." He adds, "There are just so many people out there who take the laziest version of these things. He has never done that."

It was indeed a delightful moment for me when David mentioned Tristan Walker, an incredibly talented entrepreneur who is one of the trailblazers in this book. We exchanged our thoughts on Tristan's tenacity and intellect, admiring him deeply. Our conversation took us from the early days of his career when Tristan reached out to David.

He remembered, "At the time I didn't know anything about Tristan other than he attended Stanford Business School. When he came to my office, I was taken away by his intellect and charisma. I didn't even realize he was African American before that conversation. I was so impressed by him that I asked what he would like to do over the summer. He said he wanted to intern at a place called Twitter, which had just gotten off the ground." He continued, "I knew Evan Williams, the founder of Twitter, so I emailed him, and then he hired him for the summer, which got him started."

Like Tristan, being a leader means having tremendous will and skill to be successful. That said, it also goes beyond ideas—things like charisma, your unique perspective on the idea, key relationships, and credibility building—that can make all the difference. While we hear much about how it is possible to obtain critical support for your venture from external sources, the truth remains it is ultimately up to you and me, entrepreneurs of ambition, to find it within ourselves, access those resources that bring out our best potential, and actively pursue our goals.

CHAPTER 4

MAKING BOLD MOVES: NEUTRALIZING FOUNDER STEREOTYPE THREATS EARLY

"An entrepreneur is an individual who, often against significant odds, develops and implements a unique concept for capitalizing on opportunity."

—MORRIS, KURATKO, AND SCHINDEHUTTE 2001

BUILD IMMUNITY: DO WHAT YOU NEED TO DO

Claudia crossed her arms and sighed as she spoke. "I'm of the opinion," she began, "that women, especially those of color or who are immigrants, face more barriers to entrepreneurship than their male counterparts." She paused and looked down, her voice softening as she continued. "Unfortunately, that bias also exists within us women.

Whenever I see a woman in a powerful leadership role, it's a surprise—not because I don't think she's capable, but because it's so uncommon. We need more representation, more inspiring stories that show anything is possible. That's the only way we can move forward."

In my conversation with Claudia Mitchell, a geneticist who went from struggling student to start-up founder to selling her company, she talked about how we are all so governed by these biases. Claudia went on to become a tenured geneticist at INSERM, the French National Institutes of Health and Medical Research. But just five years later, she abandoned academia and her research career to become an entrepreneur.

She cofounded and served as CEO for Universal Cells, a company developing universal donor cell technology. The Seattle-based start-up raised just $300,000 from friends and family and was acquired by Astellas Pharma in 2018 for $102 million.

Her voice raised as she said, "But awareness is the starting point here, and understanding that there are biases, but not to care for them, is the strategy that worked for me." In the case of Claudia, she decided to not care about her woman-ness, stood bold, and just went for things. As she reflected on her journey to becoming the CEO of the company she sold, she referred to her obliviousness to people who wouldn't let her grow.

She had a porcelain complexion and eyes the color of burnished hazelnuts. Her speech was even and confident, and she held her head high as she continued. "The funny thing is that, speaking of going against the current and the biases, I never really paid attention I was different than the rest. All my colleagues and fellow CEOs—most of them were male, and usually I was the only female in the room. But no matter how intimidating it was, I never let myself doubt my worth. Everyone around me was just a blur of suits and ties. My focus was always on achieving my goals instead of comparing myself to them."

Most, if not all, of us know what it feels like to be the victim of a stereotype. Whether it's based on gender, race, or even occupation, being pigeonholed into a certain category can be incredibly frustrating.

As I interviewed the people for this book, including my own experience as a woman of color, I was struck by the determination and stubbornness of each individual to just do what they needed to do.

Stereotypes will always be a part of our everyday lives. It is human nature to categorize things in order to make sense of the world around us. The problem arises when we allow these stereotypes to define how we think and act. When we do this, we are not only contributing to the perpetuation of damaging stereotypes, but we are also limiting our potential and refusing to see the possibilities that exist beyond their boundaries. We are trapped in boxes that prevent us from breaking free.

WHAT ADJECTIVES ARE YOU USING TO DESCRIBE YOURSELF?

His face radiated joy, even in the midst of difficult conversations. When asked about his journey from Mozambique to Switzerland and finally to New York, where he held positions of the highest order, he openly talked about biases and roadblocks along the way.

As a personal initiative, I developed a set of internal learning podcast interviews featuring influential leaders on their paths to power. This was designed to inspire participants of Stanford GSB LEAD. One of the guests I interviewed for the series is Bernardo Mariano Junior, Chief Information Technology Officer (CITO) at United Nations Headquarters in New York.

He is a visionary executive with twenty-eight years of international experience in senior leadership positions within the United Nations system and international organizations ranging from business transformation, digital transformation, innovation, information management and technology, cyber-security, change management, strategic collaboration, and engagement. Prior to United Nations, he was serving as the chief information officer and director for digital health and Innovation at the World Health Organization (WHO), where he led the organization's digital transformation journey to accelerate and achieve WHO's strategic goals.

Bernardo grew up in the countryside of Mozambique. His father was a civil servant, so he moved a lot. His father and mother divorced when he was five years old, and then he grew up with his father for another five years. Later, as he lost his father at a very young age, he moved to live with his mother for ten years before he went to university.

Bernardo talked about how being oblivious to his being different helped him in never having to deal with any self-limiting beliefs and actions. He remembers about a huge conference in London in 2005 about biometrics in international security after 9/11. He said, "Growing up in Mozambique, I have been extremely colorblind to my skin tone, as when I am interacting with others on such key world events, as this one, I only realize the second day that I'm the only black person here, but that didn't bother me."

In saying this, what Bernardo was also saying is that nobody gives you power; you take your own power. It is often said we are our own worst critics, and nowhere is this more evident than in the way we view our own power. The way you see yourself has a big impact on the way others see you.

If you are constantly internalizing a message of you being different, it's likely you'll communicate this to others in some way—whether it's through your body language, the words you use, or the way you carry yourself. And when others get this message from you, they're not likely to think more highly of you than you do yourself.

As a result, we may find ourselves in a self-fulfilling cycle of inaction and insecurity. Ironically, it is often our doubt and lack of confidence that prevent us from achieving the very things we desire. By recognizing our own power, we can begin to break free from this negative cycle and tap into our true potential.

Each one of us has a mental image of ourselves, and that view can affect how we behave and relate to other people. Sometimes our self-image can keep us from achieving everything we can. To better our self-image, it's useful to look at the adjectives we use to describe ourselves. Do these words reflect who we are accurately, or do they need updating?

This exercise can be eye-opening and allow us to look at ourselves in a new way. If we find the words we use hold us back from achieving our goals, we should work on changing them for more powerful ones.

POINT OUT THE BIASES TO GET A FAIRER CHANCE

Claudia recalled the many times she had been in a meeting with her ideas falling on deaf ears while her male colleagues garnered praise for almost repeating her words. As she watched her contributions go unrecognized and unheard, she thought to herself, *Is my way of expressing myself not clear enough? I said it first, but nobody noticed until a guy said it.*

Her voice rose in pitch as she said, "But I can't let that pass, because I'm so outraged by that. I would always exclaim in the middle of the meeting, 'I just said that!' Why didn't you acknowledge it or endorse it, or respond to it?'" More often, pointing to these instances, rather than letting them pass, made people aware of their biases if held unconsciously.

Bernardo points to a similar way he has been dealing with and overcame these biases through direct conversations. Without any hesitation, he is quick to answer, "In the beginning of my career, I absorbed it and said nothing, but I quickly learned that's not the best approach. Now, the first thing I do when I face these kinds of biases, or even some racist comments, I bring it to the conscious of the person who is acting one way or the other."

"Because sometimes, it's unconscious," he added with deep empathy. "So, the first thing I want to do is tap into the conscious, because I can then deal with it and discuss with the person when it is in her or his conscious mind. And by having that type of conversation, we enable a person to [know] what is the impact of what he or she said or did." He gestured with his hands as he continued, "But also, it helps me not take that home and then be sad about not having dealt with it. I learned to do that, and that has helped me a lot too."

Biases are a natural part of human cognition, and we all face them on a daily basis. While some biases can be helpful (e.g., the halo effect), others can lead to problems such as discrimination and stereotyping. Unconscious bias occurs when people make judgments or assumptions about others based on their own cultural background or frame of reference. The first step in dealing with bias is to bring it to the conscious mind of the person who is acting with bias. This can be difficult, as biases often operate at an unconscious level.

However, it is important to try to discuss the issue with the person in a non-confrontational way. By doing so, you can help them become aware of their own biases and how they might affect their choices and actions. Once biases are brought into the conscious mind, it becomes possible to address them and work toward mitigating their impact.

Absence of a conversation causes the other person to never examine their behavior. And sometimes, an honest conversation can be the difference between getting or losing an opportunity.

NO ONE GIVES YOU POWER. YOU TAKE YOUR POWER!

"The morning was still early, and it seemed like the sun had barely begun to make its presence known. The birds were already awake and in high spirits, their chattering and whistling filling the air with a cheerful harmony. The curtains were still drawn, and the morning light outside shone through the cracks to cast obscure shapes across the soft fabric," recalled Radhika Iyengar in her Interview with me.

She remembered that moment clearly. "As I was about to leave for my first day at college, I recall having a particularly poignant conversation with my late father." She paused to take a deep breath. "My father had something important to share on the realities of life. Now reflecting on that moment, I know how difficult it was for him to share his thoughts as he held my hand and said, 'Don't forget the color of your skin!'"

She paused and leaned back before she continued, "He said I might not realize this now, but I will have to work three times harder than everyone else; do three times better than everyone else and rise above." Her eyes were filled with a mix of determination and pride as she added, "That moment seemed charged with emotion and meaning, making my dad's heartfelt whisper reverberate in my heart."

Radhika's father was a gentle soul, and what he shared made her stronger. A wise and deep thinker, always observing and analyzing life around him, he often pondered the state of things. "He told me how proud he was of me, at how far I'd come." Radhika had been selected for admission to Bryn Mawr College at fourteen with full scholarship assurance. All she had to do was to affirm in her senior year of her interest and intent to attend.

Bryn Mawr is a selective women's liberal arts college in Pennsylvania. It is renowned for its academic excellence, diverse and close-knit community, and engagement with the world. She smiled as she said, "Here I was, about to start my college at barely sixteen. I entered as the youngest incoming freshman in history."

Referencing to her current endeavors, she added, "These days, I'm building my own ship and sailing it. It's not just a little ship. It's rocket ships that I think about. It's a different scale." Her father's wise yet sobering words fueled her drive and strengthened her resolve to overcome all challenges. "My father would have said today, 'Nevertheless, she succeeded.'"

Radhika Iyengar is founding partner at StarChain Ventures, a serial entrepreneur, and author of *Enterprise Blockchain Has Arrived*. Over the years, she has won various accolades and brand associations. To name a few: Top 100 Women of the Future, Web3 expert, TEDx speaker, Silicon Valley Woman of Influence, and Silicon Valley DEI champion.

As a thought-leader, she has been interviewed by *Forbes Japan*, CNN International, and *Business/Tech Insider*, and given keynotes at Google, Intel, Stanford, Harvard, MIT, UC Berkeley, Draper University, plus scores of leading international technology conferences and podcasts.

She is a member of a select task force advising California state legislature and governor news on the applications and implications of blockchain technology, and she is the founding board member of the Silicon Valley Office of the World Business Angel Investment Forum (WBAF).

BE BOLD: MITIGATE THE IMPACT OF BIAS

I sat across from Radhika, captivated by her wisdom, as she delved into the core theme of my book. She gestured with her hands, emphasizing her words. "The boundaries we're discussing here can be cultural or career-oriented. It's different for men and women, people of color and Caucasians, those who are differently abled and everyone else in between."

She offered an example to illustrate her point. "Take my cofounder, Jordan Woods, and me. We often communicate the same message, but it's received differently based on who is doing the talking. There are double standards that exist here. Women who are assertive, bold, and ambitious are often labeled as aggressive and intimidating."

Citing her own experiences, Radhika remarks, "We are expected to live up to a different set of standards than our male counterparts. When we are young, we are taught to tone down our strength, ambition, and drive so that we don't seem too pushy. Sadly, assertiveness is one of the most important assets for success, but being direct can cast us in an unfavorable light. What is seen as confident and self-assertive behavior in men can be seen as insolence or arrogance in women.

"But developing a thick skin here is what is going to define your success. Today, all that I have achieved speaks to my innate resilience, but also recognizing that continuing to keep moving forward is going to get me there. This is something a friend of mine also wrote about in her book called, *Nevertheless, She Persisted.*"

Radhika's comments are consistent with the 2003 Heidi/Howard study underscores the reality of gender bias today (Katsarou 2022). Its results suggest that women face double standards in the workforce to a greater degree than men. The idea that a woman's success can affect her likeability demonstrates that something as intangible as perceptions of attractiveness matters in the professional sphere.

This study suggests an uphill battle for successful women and implies that society continually underestimates the capability of female workers while simultaneously expecting them to prioritize likeability over success. While gentle and caring behavior generally draws positive regard, it also perpetuates a damaging gender stereotype.

Women who possess traditionally masculine traits often find themselves at a double-disadvantage—not only are such attributes discouraged, but these women may also be labelled as difficult to work with or too aggressive for team dynamics. In this way, unconscious bias limits the potential opportunities within career advancement for ambitious women exhibiting assertive behavior, as much as it affects women entrepreneurs who want to be seen as future CEOs.

Through much of history, women in particular have had to overcome a less-than welcoming environment and condescending nicknames. For example, Margaret

Thatcher, the former British Prime Minister, earned the less-than-flattering nickname "Attila the Hen" from her detractors. Similarly, former Prime Minister of India Indira Gandhi was referred to as "the old witch" by former US President Richard Nixon; and German Chancellor Angela Merkel has often been dubbed "the iron frau" due to her strong leadership style.

While these nicknames may have been intended as insults, it can be argued they act as testament to their many successes: female leaders are still seen as a threat in some circles, but this doesn't stop them from dominating with their courage and determination.

Similarly in entrepreneurship and business, studies have shown that women are perceived as too aggressive or emotional when they take charge in professional settings, while their male counterparts are lauded for exhibiting similar behaviors (Quentin 2019). Despite these hurdles, however, there have been numerous examples of female start-up founders who have defied expectations and made a real impact in their fields, whether by smashing stereotypes to win over skeptical investors or building innovative products to overcome persisting gender gaps in tech.

The bias that poses a serious obstacle for female and people of color entrepreneurs have been beaten by the likes of Sara Blakely ($1 billion net worth), Tory Burch ($900 million net worth), Arianna Huffington ($100 million net worth), Daymond John ($350 million net worth), and many others. Given the right mindset, skills, and tools, there is no reason why more women and multicultural founders can't succeed in the world of business.

GENDERED ASSUMPTIONS THAT INFLUENCE INVESTMENT DECISIONS

Does the potential of a great business model, an unbeatable product market fit, "perfect" timing, and a truly disruptive idea even matter if the founder remains invisible?

Harvard Business Review looked into the differences between the questions being asked to male and female entrepreneurs during funding competitions and the total amounts of funding raised over time. The study analyzed how "male and female entrepreneurs get asked different questions by VCs, and it affects how much funding they get" (Kanze 2017).

As part of the survey, they observed question and answer interactions between 140 prominent venture capitalists and tracked all funding rounds for the start-ups that were launched at a competition. These start-ups were comparable in terms of quality and capital needs, yet their total amounts of funding raised over time differed significantly: Male-led start-ups raised five times more funding than female-led ones.

The study elaborates that VCs would tend to ask men questions about the potential for gains and women about the potential for losses. Investors adopted what's called a *promotion* orientation when quizzing male founders, which means they focused on hopes, achievements, advancement, and ideals. But while questioning female entrepreneurs they embraced a *prevention* orientation, which is concerned with safety, responsibility, security, and vigilance (Kanze 2017). This is something we've all noticed on the red carpet when female celebrities are asked about their diets and their outfits, while male counterparts talk about their work and professional life.

This suggests that social stereotypes about gender roles may lead VCs to make inherent assumptions about how each gender thinks about risks and rewards. And these gendered assumptions can easily influence decisions about who gets funding and who does not.

As a minority founder, it is always wise to anticipate and prepare for these gendered dynamics by simply being aware, recognizing them, and emphasizing confidence in the growth potential with clear examples rooted in data and trends. Anticipating questions and coming prepared with ideas, tactics, and strategies that can redirect your answers to talk about ambition, achievements, advancement, and profit metrics can help beat this bias.

The lack of diversity among venture-backed start-ups is well-documented. According to a 2019 study by Crunch-base, nearly 77 percent of venture-backed start-ups are led by white founders, regardless of gender and education (Azevedo 2019). Just 1 percent of venture-backed founders were Black. Women-founded start-ups received only 9 percent of investments; Latino founders made up 1.8 percent of those receiving funding; while Middle Easterners totaled 2.8 percent. Asians were the second most-backed group but still with a wide gap, making up only 17.7 percent of venture-backed founders.

Lara Williams mentions in her article on Investment Monitor how venture capital companies are blind to the benefits of diversity (Williams 2021). She further states a study from Morgan Stanley that calls this "the trillion-dollar blind spot." If revenues for women and multicultural entrepreneurs were proportional to their representation in the US labor force, it would create trillions of dollars in value.

Using data from the US Census Bureau's 2012 Survey of Business Owners and the US Department of Labor's Bureau of Labor Statistics, revenue for women and minority businesses was $2.4 trillion in 2012. Had the number of women and minority-owned businesses and the portion of revenues matched their percentage in the labor force (which stood at 56 percent), then 2012 gross receipts would have increased to $6.8 trillion, suggesting a missed opportunity of up to $4.4 trillion (Stanley 2019).

Similar gendered findings show up for entrepreneurship students in that both men and women who express strong masculine gender preferences have higher entrepreneurial intentions (Gupta et al. 2009). Furthermore, due to entrenched gender stereotypes, women start-up founders are often judged more harshly than their male peers, even in cases where they display the same level of competence and success. They are more scrutinized for their mistakes and held to unrealistic standards of perfection.

And these prejudices aren't just coming from men—women themselves can be equally judgmental and unwelcoming toward female colleagues. From subtle forms of gender bias to outright discrimination, this holds true not only for women in traditionally female roles, such as caregiving or teaching, but also for start-up founders, who must navigate complex social dynamics to succeed.

One of the most pernicious effects of these barriers is that they are often unquantifiable. We can't say for sure how many great businesses never got off the ground because their founders couldn't access the funding they needed. We can only speculate about the amazing products and services we'll never get to experience because the people who could have created them didn't have the resources they needed to get started. And we can only wonder about the potential innovations and returns lost because women and people of color were shut out of the mainstream start-up ecosystem.

Luckily, due to a combined effort of personal initiative and an overhaul of existing systems, the outlook is improving. A record number of women and people of color are beginning their own businesses, and venture capitalists and other investors in their respective fields are taking them more seriously. We have a few examples in this book of investors who are creating ways to remove bias from structural and institutional perspective. But the progress is slow, as it is not a majority trend in the VC space yet.

If women and multicultural founders are to get more power to accelerate the pace of this change, they must learn the techniques and utilize the tools to counteract the influence of these prejudices. Section three presents a series of practices diverse founders may employ, as well as any founder with an aim to challenge the status quo and maximize their likelihood of success.

SECTION 3

THE TOOLKIT

CHAPTER 5

LEVERAGE YOUR PERSONAL BRAND: MAKING OPPORTUNITIES FIND YOU FIRST

"All of us need to understand the importance of branding. We are CEOs of our own companies: Me Inc. To be in business today, our most important job is to be head marketer for the brand called You."

—TOM PETERS IN FAST COMPANY

"If people like you they will listen to you, but if they trust you, they'll do business with you."

—ZIG ZIGLAR

James Clear, author and entrepreneur, tweeted about the paradox of what goes on in the minds of investors when they are deciding on their next big investment. "Investors famously look for ideas that are 'huge, if true.' But the mind is wired to believe ideas are 'true, if huge.' We trust what others trust: users, reviews, word of mouth, consensus." He shares yet another great piece of advice: "Share your work. An idea that is never spoken or written down dies with the person who conceived it" (Clear 2019).

YOUR BRAND DEFINES YOU: SOFTWARE ENGINEER VERSUS VISIONARY TECHNOLOGIST

We had met a few times before, this time in a small cafe in Basel, Switzerland. It was my first interview for this book, and I was feeling quite anxious. Taking a deep breath, I reminded myself it was okay to be nervous—it simply means you care about the outcome. He had come to Switzerland from US on a three-day work trip. A spontaneous message to meet up for a coffee turned to an evening of conversations that made its way into my book.

I saw Riddhiman Das enter the cafeteria. His hair was combed to perfection, soft yet dark brown locks glistening in the faint light. Something about this petite young man signified power and self-assurance, despite his small stature. His confidence was evident through his captivating dialogue, which held my attention as he spoke.

While discussing the themes of my book with him, I noticed his expansive knowledge on virtually any subject I brought up. His insight and intelligence shone through each thoughtfully spoken word and gesture. With soft background music and people mingling all around, the occasional interruption helped us break up lulls in conversation while providing an immersive experience that added depth to the stories he was narrating about his founder journey.

Das's intentional honesty gave me a sense of curiosity to dig deeper. He said candidly, "If you ask a person on the street in US what your stereotypical South Asian person of color will do, you will likely hear three things—doctor, gas station attendant, or computer scientist or engineer. But I'm an entrepreneur. An entrepreneur is not a gas station attendant, is not a doctor, and is not just an engineer. They may be one by backup, but they're not just one."

It was evident that since his early years, he was determined to make something out of himself and break down preconceived notions associated with people who look like him. Not only was I drawn to Das's passionate and open demeanor, but also his honest, in-your-face statements about the biases and challenges he faced as an entrepreneur.

Riddhiman Das is originally from Assam (India) and migrated to the US in 2008 to pursue his graduation. He is currently CEO and cofounder at TripleBlind, a Kansas-city based company that is taking a new approach to enterprise-level data sharing while preserving privacy. Toward the end of 2021, his current company scored $24 million. The oversubscribed series A funding was led by General Catalyst and Mayo Clinic. This round followed its pre-seed raise of $8.2 million. Mayo Clinic is continuing to expand its partnership with TripleBlind, as the health system's digital transformation arm, Mayo Clinic

Platform, plans to use TripleBlind's software to analyze patient data without seeing, sharing, or storing it and test artificial intelligence models.

As an undergraduate student, he cofounded three start-up tech companies. He worked for a start-up that commercialized the eyeprint verification system as a simple, safe replacement for entering passwords on smartphones, which was later acquired by Alibaba. He has been recognized as one of the most sought after software developers in the industry, and he has been awarded for his invaluable contribution in computer science and its application for the welfare and progress of the United States.

Das led corporate venture capital and M&A efforts for the financial services arm of the Alibaba Group. In his role as head of international technology investments, he focused on deals in enabling technologies for Alipay and Alibaba worldwide, which included blockchain, artificial intelligence, security, the internet of things (IoT), and computing.

He spearheaded the Ant Financial and Alibaba network in Israel, Silicon Valley, and New York, helping bridge the gap between the Alibaba ecosystem and technology start-ups outside of China. During that role, he surveyed the global market for trends and identified how data sharing was a fundamentally broken problem that remained unaddressed by existing solutions.

Das is also one of those examples where we see how starting early to gain recognition, awards, and contributions from reputed brands and important projects can create an impressive personal brand much quicker than many others in their field. This establishes your credibility and sets you up for subsequent success as an entrepreneur or founder. Doing something remarkable is the only thing that gets us out of the race and stand out from the mob. Making these early connections to a credible network, institutions, and projects can provide a steppingstone to larger opportunities.

His personal brand that he thoughtfully created over the years broke some of the stereotypical connotations in the US of people who look like him.

"I feel like I've had to actively fight that stereotype in my executive presence in how I carry myself, present myself, and talk about the opportunities and my own capabilities. I realized very early that when I would be at a networking event, people who didn't know me would assume I was an engineer and just an engineer. Not that that's a bad thing, but there's more to me than that. And they failed to even take the step to try to get to know me. What is it that's beyond an engineer for someone like me is something I had to curate for myself—a personal brand."

He continued, "Also, from personal experience, I can tell that as a person of color, you should know your things a little bit better than the equivalent white male person, because it is the slope of 'At what point do I call this person ignorant or incapable?' is far lower."

Das had been pointing to the research in the beginning of this book. As humans we tend to stereotype people, behaviors, and attitudes. People often think of it as something that only happens when someone is intentionally unfair. But a lot of it happens outside of people's conscious control.

This is where your intentional brand building can come to rescue. Das focused on building a brand of a technologist who did not just want to make incremental improvements to the existing software systems. He established rock-star credentials as early as in his twenties and started three tech companies before founding TripleBlind. He grew one of them—Galleon Labs—enough to become acquired in less than two years.

On his résumé, you'll find seventeen computer languages known, along with proficiency in dozens of database formats, platforms, web frameworks, and other tech tools. In 2014, he was named Technologist of the Year and worked as a developer for EyeVerify, which was named Start-up of the Year. He has also been a recipient of the 2013 White House Champion of Change by President Barack Obama.

Building a powerful personal brand is also important for entrepreneurs for various other reasons, not just for fighting stereotypes. Start-up culture is all about risk. You're pitching your entire life on an unproven idea, with no guarantee of success. It's a daunting prospect, but it's also what makes start-up culture so exciting. Start-up companies often have a lot of unproven potential. They may have a great product or service, but they don't have a track record to show their business model is successful.

You take bold bets and promise a product or a service is going to be valuable to the world. Sometimes it ends up being that, and sometimes it doesn't. But during those persevering days, you need a host of people to take a bet on your beliefs and ideas and your capacity to execute that idea—your consumers, your investors, your partners. This is where your own conviction and your own brand you build around it comes into play.

Your brand should communicate what your ideas, beliefs, and vision are and how your start-up is going to translate that unique vision to reality for the benefit of millions and sometimes billions. It needs to be memorable and reflect a level of credibility that helps you and your start-up stand out from the crowd. Of course, branding is only one piece of the puzzle when it comes to getting traction and funding. But for start-ups, it can be an important piece to grow their business.

What separates successful entrepreneurs from the hobbyists is an ability to gather and attract resources to them, rather than simply building a great product or service. You have to be extremely effective in generating publicity for yourself and your company.

In the case of Das's story, we see that he started early with building his brand and worked hard on being recognized as one of the few immigrant innovators and entrepreneurs in US. He was one of thousands nominated by the White House Office of Science and Technology policy. And he was awarded the honor because in his early entrepreneurship days, he had already filed six patents, was awarded three times, started four successful start-ups, worked at three top ten tech companies, and had been honored by Bill Gates and Google as a top student. These accolades and awards came to him, of course, because he was smart enough to deserve them; but, most importantly, because he was courageous enough to go after them and had a strong belief he deserved them.

WHAT SEPARATES THE BEST CEOS FROM THE REST

An interesting blog article and a survey by McKinsey & Company titled, "What Separates the Best CEOS from the Rest?" sheds light on why exactly the brand is so important for a CEO or founder of a company (Dewar et al. 2021). The study elaborates that if people are asked "Who's the greatest athlete of all time?" they'd probably get Michael Jordan, Serena Williams, Tom Brady, or Usain Bolt as an answer. These are iconic names that almost everyone could retrieve. However, when McKinsey did the analytics on who is the greatest athlete of all time, what they get is someone called Ashton Eaton.

"Most people haven't heard of Ashton Eaton. He retired in 2017 as the decathlon world record holder. He set the record three times in the decathlon during his career and won four world championships. But not many have heard of him. Why is that?" The study concludes that former names have significantly invested in their brand image as players as much as they have invested in their play itself.

When we similarly talk about the business world, the first names you think of are those iconic names—the Bezos, the Zuckerbergs, the Musks, the founder-led CEO companies. We have an innate attraction to celebrity, something that can be seen across cultures and spans centuries. This is in us from a very early age as we learn about hierarchies in the world and strive for recognition or attention. Today's ever-evolving media and technology have allowed such celebrity recognition to expand rapidly.

In the business world, there is a common belief the best ideas will win out regardless of who proposes them. This may be true in some cases, but as we explore in this book, how successful an idea is, and how these ideas are selected to be invested in is often dependent on who is pursuing that idea. This can be seen also in the way venture capitalists decide which founders to invest in, reinforcing the fact we are indeed drawn toward those who are perceived to be at the top of their game.

EMPLOY COMMUNITIES TO POWER YOUR PERSONAL AND COMPANY BRAND

Is there anyone who hasn't heard of Etsy? It is an online marketplace for handmade crafts today that enjoys tens of millions of members and hundreds of millions in annual revenue. Its popularity demonstrates the success of any new idea or concept is greatly dependent upon efforts of connected connectors (commonly known as influencers). These are people who are adept at using and sharing information, networks, and relationships to amplify the reach of an idea.

It all started with Rob Kalin, the eccentric founder and his idealistic approach to make commerce more human. He started with a small group of feminist crafters who were passionate about their craftsmanship and skilled at navigating digital technologies to bring it to the global market. This core group was instrumental in spreading their message across the digital landscape: connecting fellow makers, creating support communities, and growing the user base needed for Etsy's commercial success.

These digitally savvy women were integral to setting up a platform with an impact far beyond what they may have imagined when starting out. When the concept of customers interacting with sellers directly was still relatively new, Rob viewed real conversations as the most important KPI. This concept revolved around buyers and sellers communicating about all aspects of a product, including materials, the crafting process, and even the story behind the goods. Many people found this idea intriguing, as it opened up a new world of direct customer-seller interactions preceding artificial mediums such as websites and forms. To some extent, it redefined authenticity in an age where technology increasingly helped us connect without face-to-face engagement.

Without doubt, the success of Etsy can be attributed to the passionate and pioneering vision its founder possessed.

While Rob stepped down twice from his influential role, it was undoubtedly his ability to think unconventionally that propelled the success of the firm. Through dedication, zeal, and unwavering commitment, he succeeded in establishing a global peer-to-peer marketplace, which today stands strong as an outstanding example of what well thought out marketing strategy invested in communities can look like.

Etsy has an important lesson for entrepreneurs. It's essential to have advocates who believe in your cause and are willing to help you move your mission forward. Building a community of passionate people around your project is one of the most important factors for success. Not only can they become customers and collaborators, but they can also build momentum, boost morale, and bring visibility to you or your product. When creating a business or pursuing a new idea, having proponents who are dedicated to seeing it succeed gives it power and potential that would otherwise be missing.

As a founder, it's important to pay attention to how support for your endeavor builds organically, as well as consider ways to harness more enthusiasm when needed. Regardless of what that product or service might be, the course of success or failure of new ideas in business can be greatly determined by communities who take part in it. Focus on customer experience and delivering a consistent and positive outcome that reflects your brand identity and values. While building these communities, you can also engage with customers, stakeholders, and industry influencers to develop relationships and gain insights into your brand's reputation and perception.

A common question I get asked in conferences and talks, or as part of my entrepreneurship mentoring, is "Where do I start with brand building? I am not good at marketing or active on social media. I would like to work on my idea and let my work and my product speak for itself."

With any venture, it is essential to have a unique point of view that will differentiate you from other competitors. A great way to start making yourself known is to craft a brief positioning statement that conveys what sets you apart and why your product or idea is worth paying attention to.

Then, answer the question for yourself: "Why am I best qualified?" Making sure that mission is conveyed in your brand will enable you to quickly gain an audience eager to support you on your journey. An important step here (that most people often fail to do) is to strengthen credibility on executing that idea. Get associated with institutions, experts and big brands that will serve as quick heuristics. Finding ways to draw upon the unique aspects of your past can be a powerful method for engaging in any mission.

BUILD A BRAND THAT DEFINES DIFFERENCE, NOT SAMENESS

Tristan Walker's brief time on stage left a lasting impression on those present at the View from The Top speaker series session at the Stanford Graduate School of Business campus In January 2023 (James 2023). He did not come from a place of idealism or grandiose visions. He spoke candidly and plainly; speaking truths many needed to hear.

"We started selling our products in Target stores in 2016 February. In May of that year, I said, 'Let me go to Target and make sure they've put our stuff on shelves in the right way.' And I took my oldest son at the time, Avery, to the Target in Mountain View, California" (James 2023). He remembered how he put him in the cart and turned into the aisle. As they were about a quarter of the aisle down, and his son pointed to the package, where Tristan's photo was on the box.

Tristan recalled, "There's two things I thought about in that moment, knowing that my son wasn't going to realize it as a two-year-old but over time ultimately will. Number one, his dad is on the box. Particularly coming from a culture that is appreciated for its consumer influence, but less respected for our ability to produce. A black two-year-old can look at that and say, 'My dad made that,' and I can be respected as much as a producer as I am as a consumer."

"And second, we weren't in this ethnic beauty aisle with the packaging at the bottom and having it be dirty. We were above Gillette. That matters!"

"When I think about the meaning of being the first black CEO in a 180-year history, I think of that boardroom at P&G with the mahogany walled office where there's a painting of every single CEO since the beginning of time, and there are, like, fifteen paintings." You could see the pride in his eyes as he continued, "And here's a picture of me under Procter & Gamble. And I think that is the juxtaposition of what is really meaningful and powerful. Because now we're in a position to scale a free story to the world. Now he can produce. This is going to be that first painting that looks markedly different from every single other one that's on the wall (James 2023)."

"And that is a story I think our acquisition makes possible! I'm only hopeful we see more of that over time." As he said this he fixed his gaze on those below, as if to say "forget your doubts and instead picture yourself standing in my spot!"

I first came across Tristan Walker's case study as part of Professor Jeffrey Pfeffer's Building Power to Lead course at Stanford GSB LEAD (Pfeffer 2016). His case study was part of the reason I started writing this book. Tristan demonstrated that his representation had the potential to impact humanity. His remarkable achievement is a testament to how far we have come in today's society—though we still have much further to go.

As an entrepreneur-in-residence at Andreessen Horowitz, Walker was privy to invaluable resources enabling him to introduce groundbreaking marketing campaigns, which helped to spread the message further.

In his chat at Stanford with Yan James, he said, "I spent seven months wasting their time. Here's what I mean by that. I was chasing the thing I felt would make them proud to support me. It's a business school thing. I see a business model that needs disruption. Let me go do that." With a smirk on his face, he continued, "I was chasing things I had no business doing. I remember I had one idea to change the way we thought about trucking in this country. But I don't know shit about trucking."

That's when Uber was getting started. "I remember going down all these VC shops on Sand Hill Road. And a lot of these VCs thought it was a great idea and to go after it."

"And when I show up at Andreessen Horowitz, they say no, it's a terrible idea." And then he came up with several ideas, and every time Andreessen Horowitz said, "That's a terrible idea." But then Tristan's face lights up as he says, "Walker & Company was the first idea that Andreessen Horowitz said, 'That's a great idea.'" The biggest lesson he learned was how "this was the one idea they felt that I was uniquely positioned to do" (James 2023).

He emphasizes again, "I recognize that each of us in this room has something we are uniquely positioned to do! We are singularly the best person in the world to try to solve it based on our own lived experience. Usually what looks like a good idea is a bad idea, and usually what looks like a bad idea is a good idea. The problem with good ideas is that there are too many people trying to do the 'sameness.' And it wasn't until I came up with this bad idea, 'difference,' that the breakthrough kind of happened" (James 2023).

In the past, most men's grooming products in the United States had all been designed without consideration for the ethnic minorities. As a Black man, he suffered from razor bumps when he shaved, so he had firsthand knowledge of the product need. He also had direct experience with how few personal care products there were for people of color and, if available, were often consigned to the back of stores or on lower shelves. He knew there had not been money spent on product development and innovation, leaving a large, growing, and underserved market confronting products that were not leading edge.

"All of our innovations started with our own frustrations," says Walker. "If we solved our own frustrations, there were millions of people behind us who were dealing with the same issue" (Cool 2022). Walker decided to leverage his Blackness into an effective narrative that ties into his unique experiences.

Moreover, as a black entrepreneur, Walker could speak to the absence of people of color in the Silicon Valley start-up ecosystem—a topic that has drawn increasing attention as companies have become more interested in improving their diversity and inclusion. He was someone who was a talented and passionate advocate for and exemplar of the very phenomena of his business. He hired many women and people of color to design and market products for those communities.

As an aspiring entrepreneur, a person coming from a minority background may often feel like they have to "fit in" or abide by the common norm in order to be successful. But like Tristan, I believe the single most thing that makes you successful and stand out from the rest is your *difference.*

Having a unique perspective, in a world where everyone ran after "sameness," provided Tristan boundless opportunities to create value as an entrepreneur. He created an identity for himself that further contributed to the success of his business.

In the words of Tristan, "The thing I learned in my earlier stint at Wall Street was to always have a point of view, and that's something I carry with me to this day. To have a point of view in a cloudy environment is the most thrilling thing to me, because that's where a lot of the value could be generated." A clear focus and commitment to what he stood for laid the foundation for everything he did, so that everything he created had impact, direction, and purpose.

CEO = CHIEF EVANGELIST OFFICER

Barry Lawson Williams, the founder and former managing general partner of Williams Pacific Ventures, said,

"There's going to be a balance between what is intentional and what is just incidental and lucky," in his interview with Tawanda Sibanda in the McKinsey article (Dewar et al. 2021). He went to Harvard College and was the "first marshal" (equivalent to president) of his class in his senior year. He was the captain of the basketball team and went to graduate school there, receiving a combined business and law degree. Because of that background, he got a seat in the preferred section for graduation, an area reserved for distinguished graduates and large donors.

He recalls a story of this Caucasian girl who turned around and saw that he was one of the few African Americans in that section, and she said to her father, "Dad, who is that? What is he doing in our section?" And the father replied, "Oh, that's the former basketball player." Barry asserts the importance of conscious brand building in his interview. "I was in fact a basketball player and captain of the team at Harvard. But that wasn't my brand—this was an instance where I was letting people dictate my brand, not me doing it myself" (Prince and Tawanda 2022).

During his successful career, he founded and operated his own consulting and investment company for many decades, while simultaneously assuming a leadership role on fourteen public company boards such as Sallie Mae, Navient, and PG&E. While on boards, it was not unusual for him to be the lone Black member. But he managed to change the narrative about himself of that "former basketball player."

The same is relevant to founders when they are thinking about how they want to build their visibility. Choosing your "founder brand" approach is a key step in building trust with customers and prospects as well as becoming a recognizable figure. Tessa Clarke, founder of Olio, talks about how building a brand is a critical part of the founder's role. "In the early days of a start-up, it's much less about being the CEO in the classic sense and more about being the chief evangelizing officer."

She sums it up as three common approaches that start-ups should consider: the representative, the evangelizer, and the brand ambassador. The representative approach focuses systematically on matters related directly to the start-up, while the evangelizer must develop an educated opinion about related topics that circle around the brands. The brand ambassador approach is when a founder actually becomes the living embodiment of their respective brand, exuding confidence in their role both publicly and privately—like Kim Kardashian, Gwyneth Paltrow, or Elon Musk. Carefully weigh your options to ensure you make the right choice for your start-up's tone of voice and trustworthiness (Clarke 2022).

STRONG SOCIAL MEDIA PRESENCE = DEEPER POCKETS

We cannot argue with data. If founders need more proof their online presence is an important factor in raising capital, this new research should do the trick. Recent findings indicate that unicorn CEOs who are more active on social media platforms, like Twitter and LinkedIn, may be able to raise up to 20 percent more cash than their less-followed peers (Stollery 2022).

As reported in Sift's "Want to raise more cash for your start-up? Post on LinkedIn," a study crunched the numbers over sixty-five thousand articles and ten thousand LinkedIn and Twitter posts from sixty-four UK unicorns and their founders. The $1 billion-plus companies whose founders were in the top twenty most followed on LinkedIn raised an average of $938 million, more than 20 percent more than average for the total cohort. That difference was just 5.4 percent for Twitter. Founders at unicorns who got more press coverage also raised more money (Warnock 2022).

Every start-up has a story. It may be a simple one of how the founders came to an idea, or it could be a more complex tale of pivots and challenges they overcame. But no matter the intricacies of the story, if shared with investors, customers, and other members of your target audience, they increase the chance of your business's success manifolds.

It's no secret that having a robust online presence allows businesses to reach broader audiences, make amazing connections with potential investors, and build trust with stakeholders. But these statistics offer further evidence of just how powerful a tool social media can be. Building a strong and engaged presence on LinkedIn and Twitter can be invaluable for start-ups. A start-up may not have the thousands of customers needed for traditional market research, but if their founder has hundreds of thousands of followers online, this is a powerful indication that their product or service holds potential when it comes to gaining future interest.

There are also added advantages of building a social media presence. By evaluating the number of followers and the level of engagement on posts, founders can begin to better understand the needs of their target audience and how best to connect with them. Building an authentic relationship between a brand's founders and its potential customers via social media can pay dividends down the road as more people become aware.

At the end of the day, there's no better way for entrepreneurs to put their business on the map than by leveraging their terrific voices on popular digital channels. Taking the time to craft an authentic identity as a founder is invaluable in getting people more interested in what you're up to. This can range from connecting on social media platforms to creating targeted content and speaking engagements that showcase your expertise and broadcast your values. If done correctly, investing limited capital into your founder brand can equal greater benefits than spending money on expensive advertising campaigns.

JOIN, SHAPE, DRIVE THE CONVERSATION

Our conversation started like any other—polite introductions and nods of acknowledgment. But before long, it had taken a surprising shift toward an almost light-hearted tone, a stark juxtaposition compared to most other interviews I had conducted for my book.

Her curly short hair was cut to perfection and framed her cut-out jaw. Her piercing eyes gave her a look of strength and boldness. She wore a black and white striped T-shirt that had been perfectly tailored to fit her angular frame. Her enthusiasm was obvious as we spoke about building effective networks, and the eagerness in her voice made it clear that she wanted to share her knowledge and empower as many people as she can.

She spoke with the confidence and authority of someone who had seen the power of personal branding in building influential networks first-hand. "A solid personal brand and tapping into the right networks—they go hand-in-hand," she said, gesturing with her own hands as if holding an invisible wheel. "It's important to build that brand, whether it's to get onto a board or collaborate with investors or influencers. You need to raise your profile if you want to access these closed-gate networks."

My mind raced with energy as I heeded her every word. I could not ignore the immense power of developing a personal brand, which would form a platform from which to launch a successful network of meaningful connections. Influential figures begin to recognize you as a peer and are more inclined to interact. I have been firmly implementing the processes that she outlined, which has given me a huge benefit in bolstering my network in entrepreneurship and innovation.

SC Moatti talked about how she organized her insights into an approach with three distinct steps.

She moved from France to Silicon Valley to enable her dreams. Living in Paris, she decided to follow in her grandfather's footsteps and become an engineer. Through tremendous amounts of hard work and dedication, she managed to break into the internet business early on. She was also one of the first people to adopt mobile technologies, as well as blockchain. She has become an investor now, always staying ahead of the curve.

SC is the founding managing partner of Mighty Capital and president at Products That Count. She is an award-winning bestselling author and previously built products used by billions at Facebook and Nokia. SC earned a master's in electrical engineering, a Stanford MBA, is a Kauffman Fellow and YPO member, and lectures at Stanford and Columbia's executive programs.

She held her hands up, forming a triangle with her fingers, and began to illustrate her three-part framework. "You start by joining the conversation, then shaping the conversation, and then driving the conversation." She held up three fingers in succession as she spoke. "Join... Shape... Drive..." she said with a hint of emphasis.

She elaborated, "Joining really means standing out from 99 percent of people who are under the impression they are part of a conversation, being a board member or building great products, or investing, but they're really not. They're just doing the work. And there's a big difference between 'I'm an investor' and 'I'm a brand who is part of the conversation about what it means to be a great investor.' That's very different."

She leaned forward in her chair, her eyes bright with enthusiasm. "The way I recommend people get started to join the conversation," she began, "is to share a post each day. It sounds easy, but it's actually difficult. You have to be able to find quality content, and then pick the best one for the day. That means sifting through a lot of not-so-great posts so you can recognize the great ones and who's influential. That's the first step to joining the conversation—and it really sets you apart from 99 percent of the rest."

My key takeaway from this conversation with SC was that brand-building efforts not only establish credibility, it admits you into a highly exclusive club of 1 percent of true power players in the industry! Suddenly, a new world of opportunity and influence opens up.

"The second step is shaping the conversation," she said. "You don't just share the article—you give your own opinion. You can say something like, 'Deepti's article was really interesting—I especially liked section three, but it felt like there was something missing.'" She paused and smiled before adding, "My advice is to try and get on one panel every month related to the topic. Reach out to small conferences and be creative. Ask if they need a woman or a Silicon Valley perspective. It doesn't have to be about your brand. Just get out there and start getting some talking points together and create networks."

It's important to create an online presence and build a network by actively participating in social media conversations. This brave new world of digital influencers gives anybody the opportunity to become a "celebrity" through a well thought out branding strategy and gain access to exclusive networks. As highlighted above, social media allows you to connect with people in your field and become a big name in your industry.

Explaining her third point, driving the conversation, she exclaimed, "It's like what you're doing now Deepti—writing a book. You're leaving your mark on this topic for decades to come. You have a unique perspective and are challenging people to join in and contribute. That's really driving the conversation!" She punctuated her point with a friendly twinkle in her eye.

CRAFTING YOUR STORY AND TELLING YOUR NARRATIVE REPEATEDLY IS KEY

The importance of storytelling for a business cannot be overstated. Many successful entrepreneurs and CEOs have been able to win investment and secure valuations by enthusing the public about their product or concept via various forms of storytelling. Investing in a good PR team is frequently credited as having been a key factor in success; however, it is ultimately down to the leader of a company to communicate their vision effectively. They are responsible for providing the narrative, which will truly bring their product or service to life. Put simply, if you can't tell your story convincingly, you won't captivate potential customers and investors. Therefore, it is essential to hone your communication skills so that no aspect of your business proposition is left undeservedly unexplored.

As a start-up founder, a lot of your business growth depends on you getting out there and marketing it. This means going to conventions and conferences, talking with other business partners or customers, and just spreading the word to get traction with the VC community. When you're the face behind a growing business, it's your job to step out from behind the scenes. If you look at Riddhiman Das, you see how he positions himself. He is regularly featured on Industry articles, visits conferences, and makes himself available for interviews. He also writes a personal blog about topics that are relevant for his industry.

The idea is to create a halo effect. Associate with prestigious institutions, awards, or premium memberships around your topic, and have others sing your praises and the potential of your idea and company. Make yourself available to media, press, blog articles, membership communities—tell your story and repeat your story. Build credibility with thought leadership supported by data and create evidence for what you believe in through early adoption and traction of your idea.

Another way of differentiating yourself is to get others to be interested in promoting your media presence. Therefore, see if you can get a sponsorship and develop an interesting and unusual angle to how your start-up idea is driving a purpose worth caring for. Another thing that's important as it relates to brand: It's not about what you know or even what you do. A successful and established brand narrative is about persistence and consistency. It is key to be persistent using specific channels and strategies that reinforce that message and give you and your company that visibility you need. Disseminate your brand in ways that will really move the needle. Best brands are built when they intertwine the threads of personal, professional, and social priorities.

One of the great examples to learn from is Arianna Huffington, a successful author, columnist, publisher, and entrepreneur who founded the *Huffington Post* in 2005 before selling the website after just six years to AOL for $315 million. Later, she founded another online community, Thrive Global, which focuses on mental health, wellness, and behavior change through content and technology. Arianna has always had a sizable media presence and appeared on numerous political shows (Handley 2019).

As an entrepreneur, it is crucial to have a forward-thinking approach when it comes to creating thought leadership. Ensure you're not merely responding to your environment but formulating and curating planned initiatives. This also ensures you make use of your time efficiently. Scheduling topics that you can come back to again and again will provide a foundation for ongoing success, allowing you to compartmentalize tasks and filter through ideas more easily over time. Taking control of how you want to be perceived in the public space is invaluable!

Disseminate your brand in ways that will really move the needle. Aim high and push yourself. A strong personal brand can be the difference between success and failure in business. When customers, clients, vendors, and even investors see a leader with a great personal brand, they are more likely to want to do business with that company. Leaders with strong personal brands have an easier time attracting customers, partners, and media attention. They also tend to be more successful in raising capital and closing deals. Associate with prestigious awards, media, and institutions, and have others sing your praises and talk about the impact of your start-up. And, most importantly, get over your introversion and reluctance to self-promote.

Superstar entrepreneurs know that people want to engage with real people, not a company's ads about how good their products are. Some of the world's best entrepreneurs have built successful companies largely because of their personal brands. Reach and influence are key ingredients when trying to make a push for a product or service. People have to see it and have trust in the person encouraging them to purchase. Long-term influences like Elon Musk, Bethenny Frankel, and Tyra Banks have established reputations familiar enough for people to trust the cause they are passionate about. Their visibility allows them to reach more people. Their reputation backs up the content they promote so others recognize the need to support it. These individuals, much the same as Steve Jobs and Satya Nadella, are much more than just faces connected to products—they themselves act as the company brand.

CHAPTER 6

BUILD EFFECTIVE NETWORKS: PULLING MORE ALLIES INTO YOUR CORNER

"Your network is your destiny, a reality backed up by many studies in the newly emergent fields of social networking and social contagion theory. We are the people we interact with."

KEITH FERRAZZI, NEVER EAT ALONE: AND OTHER SECRETS TO SUCCESS, ONE RELATIONSHIP AT A TIME

"The richest people in the world look for and build networks, everyone else looks for work. Marinate on that for a minute."

—ROBERT KIYOSAKI, ENTREPRENEUR AND AUTHOR OF YOUR NETWORK IS YOUR NET WORTH

"Networking is a lot like nutrition and fitness: we know what to do, the hard part is making it a top priority.

—HERMINIA IBARRA, AN ORGANIZATIONAL BEHAVIOR PROFESSOR AT LONDON BUSINESS SCHOOL

THE POWER OF RELATIONSHIPS

Babu Sivadasan sat in front of me, tall and broad-shouldered, with a deep voice and an accent I could recognize from back home in South of India. His hair, the color of wet slate, was cut short around a strong jaw. He told me about the eighteen start-ups he had worked with in his thirty years of working life, many of which he founded himself. His piercing eyes spoke of the immense knowledge and insight he had gained from his entrepreneurial endeavors.

Babu leaned forward, his brown eyes intensifying as he said, "I realized the power of relationships early on when I was doing three jobs while setting up one of my first ventures, Stamps.com. I realized it didn't have to be this painful. I could get help!" Then he started investing in relationships. "Every month, I'd make a list of people I'd reach out to and build meaningful connections." He paused and shook his head. "The key thing was that I was always there for people when they asked for help. That's how I built my business—the power of relationships."

Babu Sivadasan has an impressive background of accomplishments. He cofounded Envestnet Retirement

Solutions and worked in various roles for two decades, helping countless people achieve financial wellness. Before that, he cofounded Stamps.com and served as its initial CTO, and he has been a limited partner in several venture funds. Hailing from Kerala, India, Babu's most meaningful achievement is creating roughly sixty-five thousand jobs in his home state.

He smiled as he spoke about his past experiences with business relationships. "I've always wanted to be known as a person who was good to work with in any way possible. That's the only reputation I care about," he began, his voice full of confidence. "I'm proud to say that has paid off for me in many ways. I've gained investments, support, employees, customers... you name it!"

His face lit up as he remembered his chance meeting with Vishnu, the Nexus Venture Partners investor who changed the course of his venture Jiffy.ai. The contact came through Stanford alumni. "We would meet once in a while and exchange notes." He leaned forward in his chair and paused a moment before continuing, "I originally planned to get funding from friends and family or self-fund the project entirely. We had $8 million. I didn't feel the need for a venture investor yet. I was meeting Vishnu casually for something else, and one thing led to another, and he took an interest in what I was trying to do and became an investor."

His gaze lingered on the window, and he paused to recollect his thoughts. "Twenty-five years ago, when I was starting up, it was a very different scene. There were no angel investors. There were no seed capital investors. Today, there are so many opportunities for young entrepreneurs. All they have to do is reach out and make the ask. Don't rush to a venture capitalist right away. Build an ecosystem of people you want to work with, build relationships with mentors and advisors, get credibility through them."

He cautioned, "If you go to venture investors, you take that money, you have an obligation, and they have an obligation. They want to see growth right away. Unless it is a groundbreaking idea that you're working on that has a real competitive advantage from an IP perspective, go to angels first."

He gestured as he spoke, his eyes gleaming. "Reach out to potential investors through your network. Social networks have made it easier to make contacts. Do your research and find the right fit. Understand what each investor looks for and what kind of investments they make." He added, "A good strategy is to prove yourself early. You need to progress in the first few days and talk about it publicly. That will draw people to you instead of you having to go to them."

POWER OF WEAK TIES

Asger Trier Bing looked back with a weary expression, remembering how desperate his situation had been. "I had to fly to London with our company almost out of money, hoping against all odds I could get enough funding to keep the company going. I remember sleeping on the floor of my friend's place, with water from the radiator leaking onto my feet and my shoes, and then facing the most influential venture capitalists in the tech world the next morning. Everyone wanted to get their hands on a piece of the tech market, and my business was just one of many competing for their attention."

He recalled the scene of him nervously waiting to meet with one of the top investors in London, his wet shoes squishing on the floor as he sat in the boardroom. He had gone to great lengths to secure the meetings and was determined not to let his company shut down. "Having my wet shoes on, sitting there and looking like I was asking for investment in millions. So that was getting out of my way." He had the persistence not to let his company shut down. "I was not just staying in my Danish backyard, but where the best investors were. And I did all in my capacity in those ten days to go get the meetings and talk to them."

The excitement was palpable as he spoke about his success in getting the necessary investment to start the crowdfunding platform Lendino. He explained that the platform made it easier for SMEs to access capital from banks and private investors on fair terms. He proudly reported that over $30 million had been lent through the platform, with early investments from Passion Capital and three other investors.

Asger is a serial entrepreneur passionate about how technology can help solve some of the world's most pressing problems. He has founded various ventures, including Lendino and X-Solar, a decentralized energy company bringing affordable solar power to rural Africa in Tanzania, Kenya, Malawi, and Uganda.

He spoke with disbelief and excitement as he talked about the funding they had received in London for Lendino. "They transferred the entire amount directly to our lawyer without any paperwork. It was a ridiculously high level of trust for them to give us the money like that. We couldn't believe it."

My curiosity was piqued, and I pressed Asger to discuss how they had earned that trust. I learned that trust resulted from multiple factors: the tendency to form relationships with people similar to ourselves; the founder's credibility; the idea and team that formed a solid foundation; and, importantly, weak ties. Weak ties are people you know but not very well. They're merely acquaintances. You interact with these people at work or sit in the same classrooms in university and schools.

Asger spoke excitedly, recounting the successful venture his team had closed. "We had instant credibility due to our shared alma mater, the London School of Economics, and we had gone through a warm introduction. Plus, I had proven myself an entrepreneur before, and our idea was too good to ignore. I think that's what won the trust of the investor."

AGENCY'S ROLE IN CRAFTING CHANGE AND UNITING AN EXTENSIVE NETWORK

Lisa Shu said, "It's the agency. I need to believe I have a role in the story. Because it's my story, I can't give too much responsibility to others for my outcomes or path."

Lisa has twelve years of experience in academia as a tenure-track professor of organizational behavior at London Business School with a PhD from Harvard Business School. I first encountered Lisa through the Newton Venture Program, which she had founded. From the start, she captivated me with her daring demeanor, sharp intellect, and ability to captivate her audience. So when I began working on my book, I knew she'd have great ideas to share.

Her black almond-shaped eyes sparkled as she spoke, her face framed by sleek, black hair. She thanked me for my admiration. "I'm very fortunate that I found the ideal mentors in grad school and had the best doctoral advisor. I started my career in financial services, a field with fewer templates for success, which made me more resilient. But the most critical factor in my success is the belief in crafting change, whether in yourself or your opportunities. "

I joined the Newton Venture Program, a joint venture between LocalGlobe VC and London Business School, to gain insight into the difficulties associated with diversity in venture capital. The program aims to democratize the VC ecosystem for people from typically overlooked and underestimated backgrounds, ensuring the next generation of investors represents the world we live in.

Determined to make a difference, Lisa obsessively worked to launch the Newton Venture Program in 2020, a tireless endeavor to create an inclusive environment in venture capital. Having taken a seemingly impossible task, the odds seemed insurmountable. Yet, Lisa persevered and astonished everyone with her success, leaving people wondering how she accomplished the feat.

When asked how she launched the program, she said, "Firstly, you bring a personal brand that creates a network. But it is effective if you try to gain as much diversity in that network. I didn't need to go deeper into my academic networks to start this program, meet more deans of business schools, or even bring in any of my business school relationships."

As she spoke, her mind was already connecting the dots between various networks. "I believe that the greatest opportunity lies in connecting networks that have no prior connection. Bringing together entrepreneurs, venture capitalists, and academics who specialize in this space was a way for me to achieve something big." She added, "And this venture program aimed to bring more minorities onto the main stage. It has the diversity piece, so convincing stakeholders to join hands became easy. The difference is the strength when it comes to networks. "

Lisa was talking about the idea of "filling in structural holes," a concept we teach at Stanford GSB's Building

Power class of Professor Jeffrey Pfeffer. Structural holes exist in social networks when there is a lack of direct contact or tie between two or more entities (Burt 1992). How Lisa built Newton exemplifies someone with more extensive and diverse networks who bridged the gaps and opened unique opportunities.

Lisa also talked about her frustration with the academic grind. She recounted the motivation to build Newton with hands spread wide in emphasis. "My whole career, I'd been trapped in this box, like so many of my peers. Our work only reaches small audiences. We publish in journals behind paywalls. I'm not talking about doing things like writing a book, which of course, spreads your ideas further."

She spoke with passion, her eyes glowing. "Professors are rewarded for academic research, not impact. I wanted to make more of an impact." She paused. "Newton was my way to leverage my skills and knowledge. I wanted to create an enduring institution that solves problems and has an impact on venture capital." She leaned forward, her voice low and serious. "That is my mission."

MYTH: NETWORKING SHOULD BE A NATURAL, UNDIRECTED PROCESS

Herminia Ibarra, an organizational behavior professor at London Business School, expands in her research that effective networkers focus on the long game. "A network is the set of relationships that you depend on to get things done."

The central point of Herminia's research revolves around a common misconception that networking should be a natural, undirected process. On the contrary, if we rely on relationships with people we like and get along with, it results in a "just like me" network that does not provide diversity of resources. This is because we often work in the same place, share similar ideas, join the same activities and interests, and know the same people. To truly reap the benefits of networking, you must look to weaker ties, or those more distant relationships. These people are connectors who bridge the gaps between different networks and social circles that you may not access as easily (Ibarra 2016).

The barriers to networking are often invisible, leaving many in the dark with no way to push forward. Without knowledge, it's hard to differentiate between short-term wins and longer-term investments. Networking is a two-way street—it's not just about collecting business cards, it's about understanding how relationships can be mutually beneficial in the long-term. Without this understanding, progress can feel slow, inefficient, and fruitless.

Hirminia also talks about the quality of people's network. "When I ask people how important it is to have a good network to accomplish what you want to accomplish," she began, "most people say having a good network is really important to their capacity to get almost anything done." She paused, and her expression changed to one of sly amusement. "But when I ask them, 'How good is your network as it is today?' most of the time they rate it much lower. Their networks are rarely ever as good as their importance" (Ibarra 2016).

She pinpointed the main reason for the disconnect between people understanding the importance of networking yet failing to build a real network—time! But further probing revealed this lack of priority actually came from the perception that networking was outside of their job scope when, truly, it was essential for getting tasks done and reaching goals.

She gestured her hands as she spoke, her voice gaining strength and passion as she continued. "We hold ourselves back because we don't understand that networking is a learning curve. It takes time to figure out what will reap rewards and how to use our connections for mutual benefit." She adds with emphasis, "It's about cultivating relationships" (Ibarra 2016).

Quality of network and the effort required by founders to network on a constant basis often goes unmentioned. Networks aren't created overnight. It takes approximately two years before customers trust a brand. Similarly, it can easily take years to establish a high level of trust with your network. You need to be patient and persistent to eventually build the right connections who can help you take your business to the next level.

ROLE OF SPONSORS, MENTORS, AND ADVISORS

Barry Williams highlights the role of several types of people in your network: "One should invest in sponsors. There are three types of people: coaches, mentors, and sponsors. Coaches yell at you. That's your athletic coach. Mentors listen to you—and if you're lucky, they are great listeners. Sponsors are different because they are the ones who do things for you. These types of individuals want people who are going to succeed. In a way, they want you as much as you want them." His career formula was a blend of working hard, trying to be excellent at something, and identifying a person who could help him (Prince, Tawanda 2022).

The advisors become an essential part of a start-up as they step into the role of a "sponsor." With their expertise and experience in areas such as hiring, regulatory affairs, and industry knowledge, they act as an extension of the founding team, providing essential knowledge and guidance. In case of legacy industries, like banking and insurance, they can help start-ups to understand the complexities of the business. They could also give insights into industry trends and best practices. As independent voices, they are there to ask the right questions and challenge assumptions, ensuring the success of the start-up.

Tope Awotona, a quiet, software engineer and founder of Calendly, who we will get to know more about in the next chapter, had to learn to socialize when he did not completely fit in. Having bootstrapped Calendly for years before taking on a $350 million investment in 2021, he emphasized the importance of advisors.

He said, "If you have a great concept and the potential for success, there are many investors out there who are more than willing to invest in your idea. But not everyone is a good advisor. So what I would encourage people to think about is not just who has the money, but who has the networks that will help you grow. This will help you solve difficult problems that will come along the way. It might be an international expansion, it might be people and culture, it might be product, etc. Look out for those people who can help you solve difficult problems that you will undoubtedly encounter" (Valor-Ventures 2020).

Tope wishes he had been more proactive about finding advisors for his business earlier on. Today, he says, "I have all kinds of different advisors who I lean to. For example: For people and culture issues, as you're growing a company, you need to attract people, need to retain them, you need to create a culture that makes people excited about the mission you're looking to build. I also have product advisors, engineering advisers—and also my management team functions as advisors for me. In seeking out advisors, a recommendation I have for every entrepreneur is to just start thinking about it early and also find advisors that complement them in all kinds of different ways and advisors who've solved problems you haven't solved before."

He also advises looking at building networks with potential vendors who just don't build good products, but also improve your strategy and challenge your ideas as passive advisers. Tope believes that choosing the right vendor was the difference between Calendly being successful or not. "As you're looking for people to partner with, I would encourage founders to find somebody who's just as excited about your product and your idea, not just about the money it could make" (Valor-Ventures 2020).

Creating an advisory board for your start-up and getting sponsors on board can be intimidating. It starts with making an "ask." Barry Williams illustrates this point with his own example. "None of my sponsors were sitting around losing sleep because they weren't doing something for me. They were delighted to take on this role, but I had to ask them first. I think the most important thing is to find somebody who can do something for you and package your request in a way they can come through" (Prince, Tawanda 2022). When reaching out, it's also essential to consider what you can offer the other person. Consider their life stage, goals, and other traits so you can offer something meaningful to them. This is a very important principle in networking anyway.

One word of caution, though: Be sure to avoid coworkers, vendors, or contractors on the advisory board, even if they have the necessary skills. The most important quality for a board member is emotional detachment. Remember to strive for a harmony between listening to counsel and trusting your own instinct.

PEOPLE GO AROUND AND SAY, "WHO DO YOU KNOW?

"There's going to be a balance between what is intentional and what is just incidental and lucky. One needs to develop own network so you can position yourself to be lucky," said Barry Lawson Williams, founder of Williams Pacific Ventures, while discussing the role of several types of people in your network (Prince,Tawanda 2022).

It takes hard work and dedication to gain access to top-tier investors who are often inundated with requests for meetings and pitches. You have to intentionally place yourself to be lucky. David Hornik of Lobby Capital emphasized this point in our conversation. "I am very quick to say the very best way you can get funded is to be introduced to great investors by people they know and trust."

In line with David's comment, if you ask most people what the best way to get meetings with investors is, they'll answer with one word: warm introductions. VCs consider portfolio founders, advisors, current investors, board members, and people from the most recent round of fundraising as the most sought-after referrers. Of course, there's also the option of asking for intros from acquaintances if you have no other option. But that's a risk, since you can't gauge how the investor feels about them or what they think of you and your business.

FINDING YOUR WAY "INSIDE"

As I ask Swapna about the obstacles the venture capital industry places on female VCs, she wrinkles her brows. "It's undoubtedly present," she says, her voice dropping to a low, calculated tone. "The fact that you are still a minority. Your contacts appear very different"—her response gains momentum—"which is analogous to why we wind up investing in more women founders, since our network looks like that. It's various." She goes on, her voice slightly louder. "But if you take a look at the venture capital group, it's all men. They naturally lean toward investing people they are familiar with."

Swapna often reflects on the extra effort she has to put in to build her professional network, which is 95 percent men in VC Industry in India. She regularly reaches out to her peers in the industry to grab coffee, join forces on projects, or just connect. She understands many of them have existing networks and don't rely on hers, while she needs those networks to succeed. "They don't need a platform called Swapna, while I need that 95 percent of the network." But the fact is, it is possible to break this boundary if you insist. It boils down to having that awareness and accepting you are outside and finding your way inside.

As it relates to minority founders, David emphasized with his deep-throated voice, "I think the stories of under-represented individuals go unheard, much more often than connected white men. And that's a challenge of access that the whole community has to solve." He adds,

"The first-generation students or entrepreneurs who are from communities where there isn't a lot of wealth or connectivity, or engagement with the broader venture community—it's difficult to be able to tell their story if they don't have this initial introduction."

David and Swapna's insight is something that most in the venture community recognize: Navigating a network where social capital is held disproportionately has left many entrepreneurs without a platform to tell their stories. Building a network is hard; building close bonds is even harder as we are more likely to connect to those like ourselves; and it is difficult to find commonalities.

However, if you're trying to access these social circles of "networking elite" and "venture capital communities," there are a few tips and tricks that can help you get closer to that goal. Of course, social media has been a great equalizer. Regardless of where you come from or what resources you don't have (e.g., prestigious schooling), any person can create an account and start building relationships with influential people.

Some ways are what we discussed in chapter on building a personal brand. Focus more on what you stand for than promoting a product or company, e.g., SC Moatti's "join, drive, shape" framework, and David's VC blog to build, credibility, visibility, and influencer network. Target and associate with relevant brands and events for networking. Remember sociological principles like introducing yourself at events to generate word-of-mouth interest.

David also added another example of how one can utilize secondary network of VCs: "I speak at lots of accelerators and incubators. If you're part of those programs, then there's an opportunity to connect. Getting into those programs at least has a broader application process. And so that may be your path to engage in this broader community."

The other example he gave is about grabbing the opportunity when you see it. "There is a woman who I met at Stanford during a class I teach on. She boldly asked and signed up for a dinner at my house with a bunch of other kids, and we had a great conversation. Any one of my students who had reached out to me I would have spent time with them and would have continued helping them. But she was the only one who did something audacious like this, and then she started a business during the pandemic." He smiled. "She reached out to me again and has continued to get my help."

Chris Smith suggests targeting lesser-known venture funds instead of big brands for successful networking. He added, "They all want to be backed by Sequoia Capital! But one of the most positive elements happening in venture capital, where US is ahead compared to the UK, is rise of the emerging fund managers from diverse backgrounds." From a founder's point of view, specifically if you're outside this whole VC bubble, you don't necessarily have to get inside through a tier one fund. You can do it through any kind of emerging manager and build those connections.

He uses an example to illustrate working with accelerators and incubators as a strategy. "I have an interesting story about Vinehealth. It's an oncology application. And the two founders, Rayna and Georgina, are actually the reason we started the 'female founder office hours.' Because when they sent us the press release to announce the round, it said that one penny in every pound goes to women founders. And we sat in the office in disbelief for a long time, checking it, googling it, and that was right. They were doing this because there were so many women founders like them who had amazing ideas and backgrounds but couldn't access capital." They inspired him to start doing something in this area.

He explained how the founders, who had both worked in the NHS and had strong technical backgrounds, did not have access to venture capital before. But by joining a well-known incubator and accelerator program in the UK, they were able to participate in a demo day, exposing them to each of the top UK VCs in a single pitch event. "So this is an incredibly powerful route for first-time founders to get incredible distribution, as long as the equity giveaway and the terms are appropriate for people coming from outside the ecosystem."

He offered another perspective in how VCs themselves are changing to allow more diverse founders to be heard easily and get access—the changes that are happening at institutional side, although not to the same extent as desired.

He said, "I hate this notion of needing a 'warm introduction' to get access to VCs. It should be open to everyone so the best possible founders can build the most exciting companies, regardless of where they come from. Playfair Capital is taking steps to make this happen. We have an open pitch form on our website, where we guarantee to founders we'll get back to them within five days. Some of the best investments we've made has been through cold inbound."

He also gave some more details about women founders' office hours: "It is an initiative to bring together investors and women founders that we started in 2019 at a very small scale in our office. We had about fifteen investors and thirty founders come together for fifteen-minute pitching-mentoring sessions." He said proudly, "We're now on our ninth edition, and the last one had 150 investors and four hundred founders from across the UK, Europe, and in MENA."

He added, "You can get access to us anyway, but I think in the market, it still helps to build those connections and networks for success with the larger investor market, which is still closed doors."

Dan Mathies of Reaction Fund also says, "We've had a very diverse portfolio. We were very proud of the kind of diversity that we have. But at no point did we go out and make that a goal. It was an outcome based on meritocracy."

There is a shift in VC mindset. They are interested in building their deal flow and increasing their trusted network, no matter where it comes from. They're not just looking to write a check to the first entrepreneur they meet.

Tope Awotona of Calendly suggested "bootstrapping" as a way of "finding-your-way-in." He argues that raising money later on in the life cycle means giving away a smaller equity and keeping more control. One of the examples of his idea's worth was a comment from Blake Bartlett, a partner at OpenView Venture Partners who invested in 2017. "Scheduling tools at the time were focused on lots of bells and whistles, but Calendly provided an Instagram-like experience for a business tool. And it was viral." Before approaching potential investors, he made sure the product was attractive enough to generate enough sales and interest they could not say no to. Where he also excelled is on building long-lasting meaningful relationships with investors who have more to give than just money (Shen 2020).

COLD EMAILING: HAVE YOU DONE YOUR RESEARCH?

David pointed out the importance of homework and research for founders who lack a warm introduction to investors. "I look at every email I receive, and my email is widely circulated. Anyone can find it. It's not hidden." He then suggested, "You can send me your executive summary along with a brief description of the business. Though I'd have to say that's a rather uncreative approach and doesn't merit my attention, I'll still consider it."

He stresses the importance of engaging with investors on a personal basis and provides tips on how to use already-accessible information to build relationships with potential investors. He added, "The email that makes me actually pay attention is, 'Hi, David or Mr. Hornik, I was reading on your blog where you wrote X, Y, and Z... I am building something similar,' or it could be 'I saw online a video you had recorded talking about your dyslexia. And it resonated with me because I'm also dyslexic.'" An email with a meaningful reference to his blog, video, or purpose can make his ears perk up.

He explains how personalized evidence of values and interests can engage investors and make the difference between having one's proposal considered or ignored. He leaned in, his eyes intent and piercing. "In these examples, I may not know much about you, but you've taken the time to know me, and you've taken the time to figure out why it is that 'who you are' and 'what you are building' has any resonance with me." His voice was firm but kind. He paused and said, "But if your introductory pitch is a grand plan for a multi-billion-dollar market, then I'm not even going to get to that until I've established if I can trust and work with you."

Swapna Gupta of Avana Capital commented that when someone reaches out to each team member on LinkedIn, it shows they have done their homework. "But I think the other thing founders can do, and that rarely comes up, is to make a direct reference," she said as she tucked a strand of black hair behind her ear and leaned forward in her chair. She added, "The best way is to reach out to a founder we've already invested in. When we invest in a founder, we invest in a family. A family will not send you crap. So, we trust the contact coming to us is already vetted in some sense!" She nodded and added with emphasis, "Any founder who has reached out to other people in our network who we know would always be top of mind."

She offered another perspective, "You might also want to create FOMO (fear of missing out) in investors, but with all the right and genuine information, or else it doesn't work. When that email comes from a founder we do not know, does that email have enough meat for us to warrant our attention?"

She said it goes back to the founder being a great salesperson above all. "It could be as simple as the next path breaking technology or a mind-boggling traction. Or it could be even something as simple as my round is closing, something there to bring that fear of missing out." She candidly added with a smile, "We are all very prudent investors and we want to do the right thing, but there's also a real fear of that one unanswered email amongst VCs, which could be the fear of missing out on a Google." With her continued honesty she mentions, "One thing which people should know about this venture industry is people always read their emails. You just need to get them to respond your email."

"Perhaps it's a UK thing, but some founders are shy of chasing up," said Chris with a rueful smile. "I always recommend to founders to treat follow-ups like the three-strike thing. If you send an email, and you don't get a response—chase once, chase twice, and the third time."

He paused to let that sink in, then continued, "The reason VCs don't respond is not because they're not interested. It's because the inbox is really full, or they're in the middle of closing an investment. I believe our lives as VCs are so many times easier than it is being a founder, but we get pretty busy sometimes. That's why I encourage people to chase. You send them an email a week later, they're a bit quiet so they pick it up and they get back to you. It goes back to the importance of resilience."

To give some examples of his investments that came through cold inbound, he talked about Protex AI, for which they recently raised a series A that was a cold inbound. Continuum Industries is based up in Edinburgh that was a cold inbound via LinkedIn. He added, "This is an example I used in a blog post about once being followed by the founder chasing me around a conference venue to do a demonstration because I happen to have a Playfair Capital T-shirt on. About five out of twenty-five investments have been cold inbound. From our perspective, there's no issue; however, the market has not moved totally in that direction."

Dan Matthies said, "Before I take a meeting, I look at the person's background. If somebody reached out who I don't know, I check their LinkedIn and look for common connections. And if there is no one, I look at their company's LinkedIn page." His mouth quirked into a half-smile. "And if you have three followers on your company page, and you wrote in your email that this is the biggest opportunity, I am wondering, Why are other people not clamoring around it?" He gave a dramatic pause. "The excuse you often get is that they are in stealth mode. But that is not true, because, you know, they're not the stuff that they're talking to you."

I wanted you to listen to the voices of the investors in above comments and believe! Cold emailing can and does work. And the only reason it doesn't work is because you haven't put in enough work into crafting that email. If you lack access to an already existing powerful network, you can still reach the highest tiers of investors. From India to the UK, East Coast to Silicon Valley, humans everywhere are the same, as we see in the above examples.

The successful founders are intentional and strategic in their approach and dedicate the extra effort needed to research the individual they are contacting. They resonate with them, whether through shared values, emotions, or purpose, and eventually find their way in!

There is clearly still value in getting access through warm introductions. It is more likely, at least, to get your deck read. But going cold with good research, idea, founder's background; or using social media to influence your personal brand and hence interest of investors in your company; or through accelerator and incubator programs—these are few of the alternate routes available to founders as well.

Here are some strategies to pull more
allies into your corner:

STRATEGY #1: USE SOCIAL MEDIA AND SPEAKING ENGAGEMENTS.

Use the join, shape, drive framework to build a personal brand and get noticed by investors, advisors, and mentors. As a bonus, through all these activities, you'll be able to build a following of people who believe in your mission and provide you with traction.

STRATEGY #2: USE NETWORKING PLATFORMS.

From FoundersList to Indie Hackers, Y Combinator's cofounder platform, Soho House in the US, and even more, there are countless online and offline platforms to connect with other founders. These networks appear all around the world, so no matter where you live, you're sure to find a hub. By meeting five or six founders each week, you'll have around twenty or more potential referrers after four weeks.

STRATEGY #3: GET TO KNOW FOUNDERS IN YOUR INDUSTRY.

The approach mentioned earlier is an excellent option, but there's no assurance that founders you meet will have investor connections. A better approach is to contact the founders of relevant companies that have achieved one to two steps more success than you have. They can give you some professional advice and introduce you to the people who funded their business.

STRATEGY #4: BUILD A POWERFUL BOARD OF ADVISORS.

They do not just help you with the product and business mentoring. They also build your credibility as a start-up at the same time. Influential ones are most likely connected to wide network of investors too.

STRATEGY #5: BE PART OF ACCELERATORS AND INCUBATORS.

This gives you access to multiple investors through single pitch or demo events. They are also great for connecting with their founder alumni, who could eventually become your referrers.

STRATEGY #6: WRITE COLD EMAILS AND USE LINKEDIN.

As demonstrated, this strategy works; yet, sending the same message to each investor won't get results. Investors tend to be more likely to respond to communication that is tailored to them. Furthermore, always conclude your emails with a call-to-action. If you have raised money in the past, mention it to create a sense of fear of missing out (FOMO). Nothing creates this feeling better than having other investors demonstrating loyalty to investing in you. And absolutely do not shy away from "chasing."

STRATEGY #7: GO WITH EMERGING FUND MANAGERS.

Forget getting to the top of the mountain and focus on the lower peaks. Diversify your network, and look for the venture funds that are overlooked.

STRATEGY #8: FIND INITIATIVES THAT ARE GEARED TOWARD MINORITIES, WOMEN, OR FIRST-TIME FOUNDERS.

Venture capital firms are beginning to explore new ways to discover untapped investors and founders from underrepresented backgrounds. They are setting up sidecar funds, organizing pitch competitions, circulating office hours listings, and eliminating the need for introductions while making the whole process quicker and more transparent. Make sure to do your research and stay connected with other entrepreneurs to be aware of potential investment opportunities.

STRATEGY #9: BE PART OF EVENTS AND CON-FERENCES.

It's important to remember you don't have to attend every networking event. Instead, focus on the ones you think are most important and give them your full attention. Most people I know view networking as a chore, but it doesn't have to be. I suggest coming into the event with an attitude of curiosity. Think about who the people are, what you can learn about them, and what they can learn about you. This can make it much less of a dreaded task. Rather than just attending a conference, consider organizing a panel to interview a relevant speaker for your start-up's industry, or doing a presentation as a speaker on your mission and vision. This may involve extra effort, but the returns are greater. More people will be aware of who you are, what idea you're working on, and what you're building, and they'll be more likely to reach out.

STRATEGY #10: ADD VALUE TO YOUR NETWORK.

Don't just stop at the first email, connection, or meeting you have had, even if it did not go as expected. An effective way is to add value to your network regularly. It's using a mindshift about networking—it's not just what your network can do for you but what you can do for the people you're connected to as a result of the network you have developed.

Start-ups can provide value to venture capitalists and other investors in several ways. Some examples include:

supplying a solution to a problem faced by the VCs or their portfolio companies; presenting the VCs with fresh business opportunities, partnerships, or customers; displaying expertise in their field, market, or technology; showing how their venture can create synergy with the VCs' existing portfolio companies; or making proposals that can improve processes, heighten efficiency, or cut down costs.

Founders should also bear in mind that their network has the potential to be of great worth to investors—by granting them access to their resources, technologies, or connections that can benefit the VCs and their portfolio companies, or showing how their project can form collaborations with other organizations, universities, or research organizations that the VCs may appreciate. By supplying value to investors, start-ups can stand out from other possible investments and increase their chances of securing funding.

STRATEGY #11: CREATE A DIVERSE NETWORK AND AIM FOR CENTRALITY.

Take the time to meet new people and establish a vast, diverse network. The people who serve as hubs of communication, or the centers of the network, are viewed as more influential. If you become connected to them, then it increases the chance you will be viewed as highly connected too. This is something we saw in the case of Lisa Shu and how she used diverse networks to tap into a unique opportunity and became central in minority founders' network.

STRATEGY #12: GET CREATIVE IN FINDING WAYS TO MEET PEOPLE.

Investors often back people they like, so it is beneficial to create a connection with them. David Hornik shared how he invested in a start-up that was linked to his personal struggles with dyslexia. I also use my own example where I was able to get in touch with an influential leader through my passion in photography, offering to help his daughter pursue it as a career. Another example is when I wanted to meet a leader who visited Switzerland for the first time. After researching his profiles, I found out he was a hiker, so I sent him references of good places to hike.

Don't just try to meet people at events and conferences but also through common interests, activities, and clubs. According to Keith Ferrazzi, a master networker, passions and events you organize around them will create a deeper level of intimacy. Consider volunteering, doing workouts, having a book-signing party, or attending theatre events. Establish a common interest with the person you wish to connect with (Ferrazzi and Raz 2014).

STRATEGY #13: BUILD ON WEAK TIES.

Weak ties are not just important for getting connected to investors or other founders. If investors decide to back you, they will likely do some research into the people you've worked with in the past. You must not only form new ties, but also nurture your existing ones. Reach out to distinct persons, in particular, past classmates, former colleagues, ex-supervisors, and clients. These people were once strong ties and can vouch for your skills and capabilities.

STRATEGY #14: LOCATE PRIVATE INVESTMENT CLUBS.

Find the people who hold the resources and investments to help your start-up or those related to them, and build relationships to get into their circles. Information on funding rounds and competitions or campaigns is shared in small networks, making it hard to track down these opportunities in time to apply. These groups can also act like close-knit investment circles, where the money continually circulates among the same participants. If you want to get to these sources of investors and funding rounds, you need to join the club.

STRATEGY #15: NETWORK TO BUILD RELATION-SHIPS, NOT TO RAISE MONEY.

It's really important you think of your networks not just to get money, but everything that you would need for your business to grow. You don't want to be a "hot deal" that's simply being thrown money because investors think you'll be profitable. You want to have investors who are convinced of your market, your offering, and your team. The best investors for you are those who have a deep conviction in what you're doing and who believe in your vision. They're the ones who will be the most supportive and helpful as you grow your business.

Holding your breath, you can sense a great weight surrounding you. This chapter is the longest of the book and one of the most integral. In my eyes and in the eyes of countless founders and investors, mastering these skills are crucial to make it in this unforgiving industry. If you are to take away anything from this chapter, let it be this:

- Networking is one of the jobs of a founder. Radically change how you spend time in building your vision.
- Be strategic and deliberate in your networking efforts.
- Networking is not a skill we are born with. We can increase our efficiency and become more effective, cultivating relationships through practice.
- Our influence is a by-product of who we're connected to, how much they trust us, and the sense of community we share.

CHAPTER 7

PERSIST A LITTLE LONGER: FOCUS, DETERMINATION, AND WILL TO SUCCEED

"The ones who are crazy enough to think they can change the world are the ones that do."

—STEVE JOBS

"The only limit to our realization of tomorrow will be our doubts of today."

—FRANKLIN D. ROOSEVELT

WHAT YOU DON'T GET IS WHAT YOU END UP CREATING

After studying in Patna, India, Shradha was proud to be admitted to St. Stephens college in Delhi, which is one of the most difficult colleges to get into in the country. At the college, she quickly learned of the debating society, a club where students could hone their speaking skills, and applied to be a member. To her dismay, however, she was denied soon after. The intricacies and protocols of debating had taken her off guard, leaving her feeling discouraged and overwhelmed.

"I thought I could speak very well, and I didn't get selected. They told me a hundred things about dialogue debating, and different kinds of debating techniques that I wasn't aware of" (Sharma 2015). She thought back to her days growing up in Bihar, one of the Indian states judged most harshly by metropolitan cities. She knew that their schooling was not on par with the systems in those metropolitan areas, and she instantly felt the sting of it.

She went back to one of her teachers in Bihar to tell her, "We have so many limitations. We are not exposed to the right kind of things in schools here." She conveyed to her teacher how she was finding it difficult to compete with other students in Delhi because her school in Bihar did not prepare her for that. And the answer from her teacher changed her perspective for life that made her resilient about succeeding in all endeavors, including YourStory, the business she started in 2008.

Much like an anchor from which she could draw strength and hope, these uplifting words of wisdom motivated and inspired her toward success. "Sometimes we don't get what we want in life, but that is exactly what fuels us to work harder for it" (Sharma 2015). The words stayed with her throughout her journey and pushed her to achieve what seemed like the impossible. Since that day, every attempt to reach for the stars would bring her one step closer to her goals. "I was very hungry, very thirsty, very desperate all my life 'til today. I am always looking at the opportunity and not the constraint" (Sharma 2015).

Shradha Sharma is the founder and chief editor of Your-Story, "stories about start-ups and entrepreneurships," and she is driven to make stories and start-ups matter. She started this venture because of her deep belief that India's new-age entrepreneurs deserve to have their stories heard. She has scaled YourStory to become one of India's leading digital media platforms, with inspirational storytelling at its core.

Shradha was featured on *Fortune*'s list of the "Best 40 under 40" entrepreneurs in India for three years in a row. In 2018, she won the *Forbes* Power Trailblazers award and was twice featured on LinkedIn's list of powerful influencers, along with Prime Minister Narendra Modi and actor Priyanka Chopra. With more than two million followers on her personal social media handles, Shradha's influence is far-reaching—one that she has leveraged to shine light on businesses such as Ola and Paytm much before they became unicorns.

Shradha has been an extraordinary inspiration for me over the past three years. Her courage and passion to tell her story and other entrepreneurs' stories in India have resonated with me. I knew her resilient attitude to entrepreneurship was the kind of narrative that deserved attention—and, more importantly, needed to be shared and included in my book.

During my research, as I was going through endless articles and videos of her on the internet, nothing could have prepared me for the video that caught my attention. She was neither highlighted nor glamorous, but her presence and bearing screamed of strength and confidence. She strode onto the stage smiling proudly, dressed in an unassuming Indian outfit of black with a green stole. Her entrance sent shockwaves of applause and cheers flooding through the audience as people stood up to acknowledge her arrival. She was invited for a fireside chat. She sheepishly admitted her trepidation, though clearly there was a strong sense she knew she was in good hands with interviewer Sandeep, her friend.

"I remember I called my mother once to Patna and told her that I quit my job and I want to start my business. And she started crying on the phone. And I was wondering, *Why is she crying? When actually, she should be happy that I'm going to become an entrepreneur*" (Maheshwari 2023).

She was motivated by a combination of factors. Fear of failure drove her on, determined not to let her mom down. But her ambitions extended beyond simply proving she could do it. She wanted to do something positive and meaningful. "Positivity is a habit. It's like brushing your teeth. And I was definitely not one of those people who would run away from what I had started" (Maheshwari 2023).

She felt drawn to the idea of sharing stories about rising start-up founders in India and spreading awareness of their work. Despite the negativity she had seen in her life, she wanted to make something good out of it that would resonate with others as she calls it "the ability to appreciate each other."

"I think what is very important is the very first step, you have to come and stand on the stage." She reflects on how she got started with a website with few text stories and photos of entrepreneurs to a business today valued at $40 million and her channel with fourteen million followers and about five million subscribers. "I didn't even come from a tech background. Building a website in 2008 with no website making platforms like today—it was hard. I went to IIT school in Mumbai to get two students to make my website in return for free Indian snacks for lunch" (Maheshwari 2023).

Despite her enthusiasm and readily available platform, it proved challenging for the young entrepreneur-journalist to find consistent subject matter. Most of the founders she reached out to required convincing. After all, she was just getting started and hadn't yet made a name for herself. But once she had the first traction, things grew, like network effects with verbal viral marketing without any employed advertising campaigns. She soon found considerable success in finding inspiring figures to write about—yet it was not without its share of hardships.

She recalls an incident from her early days of starting the blog. She had been so sure of herself and her goals when she entered the office of a gaming industry entrepreneur to request an interview. She was hoping to learn more about his story for a feature. Yet, despite her years of experience in prominent news media such as CNBC and *Times of India*, and all the professional contacts she had so carefully built within the industry, those credentials did not seem to be enough for him. There were also moments of sadness along the way that arose from the lack of help from her industry contacts and relationships.

It was crushing at the time, but it served as a powerful lesson in perseverance that informed much of her entrepreneurial journey and helped shape her into who she is today. She remained steadfast in her goal and clung onto hope that eventually things would turn around. Happily, they did.

Few had the foresight at that time to recognize the potential in their stories, but Shradha could see what others did not. "Once you have the trust, goodwill, brand, data, and insight, then making money from your business is an easy thing" (Maheshwari 2023).

She recalled how her business took jumps after her very first encounter with one of the interviewees she was writing about. "I still remember the name of the entrepreneur, Bakshish Dutta of Sun Microsystems, which is now acquired by Oracle. He asked me how I make money from these stories, and I had no answer. I was living on my savings for the past year to bring these stories forward." Her face lit up as she said, "He gave me $100,000 to run a program campaign on my website to enroll people for start-up essentials program. From that point on, I could prove to the world that monetization of these stories and ideas was possible and my business was profitable (Maheshwari 2023).

"An interesting thing that I did was I disrupted the business model. I did not try to make money from ads. That's what everybody else does." She sheds further light on what made her business profitable and how she continued to make it a sustainable and a viable business. "Even though the front end of the business was B2C (business to customers), telling stories to the audience, the back-end model was B2B (business to business). I realized I was collecting a lot of data and intelligence that started building in the background because of the stories I was sharing. So I started working with the journals and trade bodies" (Maheshwari 2023). In 2010 she also started working on events like SheSparks and TechSparks, which not only generated income but also enabled quite a bit of momentum for YourStory. She also added revenues through research reports, newsletter subscribers, and video series like "Money Matters," "C Suite with Shradha Sharma," and more.

Her story is one of fierce dedication in the face of looming prejudice. Yet through her innate determination and the unwavering support of her early allies, she was able to break through barriers that were long scripted against her. She proved to the world that regardless of how you were perceived from the very start, with enough drive and ambition, nothing can stop you from achieving your goals. By striking through pernicious clichés about class and gender, she showed that feeling ashamed or forced down by adverse obstacles had no place in her narrative, instead using these challenges as prompts to test the uncompromising boundaries of what was possible.

She stands tall on the stage of Josh Talks as she says, "What does the hardest moment give you? What does it leave with you? If you think back, you will see that despite all, we are still standing! We are better. We are evolved. And we are very proud of that experience. We were not proud when that experience happened. But we are very proud that it happened. Because this is what shaped who you are today" (Sharma 2015).

BOOTSTRAPPED TO UNICORN

As the founder of Calendly, an all-in-one meeting lifecycle, a modern scheduling platform that helps individuals, teams, and organizations automate meetings, Tope Awotona has an effective narrative of his determination and passion. He was no software engineer. He had the business mind with an idea that needed software developers to build his vision. At that time, he needed a business in Kiev, Ukraine, to help him build out the tech behind his scheduling software company.

"I was scared," he confessed, recalling the sounds of explosion and chaos barging into the confines of his hotel room in Kiev, a mile or two from the center of the riots where protestors at one point set up a ring of fire to ward off police officers. "But Calendly was my life. I felt like I had no option" (Shen 2020). Tope found himself caught in the midst of international tension when he traveled in 2014 amidst the Ukraine crisis. Despite warnings from his friends and family, he chose to fly there nonetheless, as he wanted to be sure the country was stable enough to sustain a long-term business partnership.

The situation had escalated into the bloodiest chapter of violence since protests had initially erupted, with thousands of riot police trying to regain control of the city. This made for a tense arrival for Tope, but it ultimately paid off. Having hired a software team based in Ukraine, Tope was determined to observe and assess first-hand if this partnership would endure amidst the chaos and danger surrounding them.

"Looking back, it was probably stupid for me to go. But it was also this single-mindedness that has helped fuel Calendly's remarkable rise." Tope's statement perfectly illustrates the internal drive and passion one must have to become a start-up founder. "It's not enough to want to start a business. That's not a strong enough reason to start a business. The strong reason to start a business is that you're passionate about a problem and that you're dedicated to devoting a significant part of your life, really, to solving that problem" (Shen 2020).

Despite his turbulent childhood in Lagos, Nigeria, Tope Awotona did not allow it to define him. As the second youngest of seven siblings in a lower upper-class neighborhood, Tope grew up with the daily fear of extortion and violence. This fear became reality when he was twelve years old. That's when a group of men followed his father home and demanded access to his car.

His father threw them the keys, and tragically, they shot him regardless. The shooting left Tope with post-traumatic stress disorder and chronic insomnia that still persists to this day. Despite living through such trauma, Tope was motivated by the perseverance of his parents. His father was a microbiologist and entrepreneur, while his mother worked at the Central Bank in Lagos. He used this resilience born from hardship to ultimately become successful in life.

At the age of fifteen, he moved with his family to Atlanta, Georgia, US. He studied computer science at the University of Georgia, then switched to business and management information. According to David Cummings, founder of Atlanta Ventures, which led a $550,000 seed investment in Calendly seven years ago, "Tope could be the most successful African-American tech entrepreneur of his generation" (Feldman 2022).

Tope Awotona is a rarity in the unicorns landscape. Founded in 2013, Calendly transformed what used to be a time-consuming scheduling nightmare into a simple process thanks to advanced automation features. By taking busy work off peoples' to-do lists, Tope was able to create a comprehensive solution and achieve incredible success that turned into a $3 billion start-up. Additionally, Tope put Atlanta on the unicorn map as one of only three companies founded by a Black person that reached valuations of more than $1 billion at the time of writing this book—Compass (valued at $6.4 billion), Zume (roughly $2 billion prior to the pandemic), and Calendly ($3 billion).

"Initially it was for financial reasons. I literally needed to pay my bills," he says. "But the motivations have shifted over time. As Calendly has grown, I just get a lot of people who don't fit the mold who reach out to me, who are women, men, people of color, who have been so inspired by the story. That keeps me going through the tough days" (Shen 2020).

When Tope Awotona developed Calendly, it truly seemed to be a case of the right idea at the right time. His desire to turn his vision into reality was so great that he used all his personal savings to get the business off the ground. His desperation to solve an issue he had been suffering from himself made him obsessed with finding a solution, which would ultimately become one of his biggest successes.

This keen eye and ambition may have come in part due to earlier failed ventures that allowed him to develop practical insights. When asked about how crucial passion and commitment were in achieving success, Tope said, "If starting a business is just about making money, it'll probably be very difficult for you to succeed because you can't fake the passion" (Pompliano 2021).

Awotona, now forty-one-years-old, is a prime example of an entrepreneur who embraced the bootstrap lifestyle until his idea was ready to be developed into a minimum viable product (MVP). He had a tough decision to make.

He had an idea for a business he believed would succeed, and he had decided to sacrifice a stable job at the sales department of cloud services company Dell EMC; empty his retirement fund; max out credit cards; and take on expensive small-business loans in order to pursue his business venture. Surprisingly, Tope now considers the lack of available funds early on in the process as a benefit that directly contributed to his success.

His professional journey began in the world of technology, where he held sales positions for companies such as IBM, Perceptive Software, and Dell Technologies. Seeking entrepreneurial success, Tope decided to pursue his own start-ups—although these attempts at launching a business of his own were eventually unsuccessful. Subsequently, he turned his attention to the online calendar scheduling industry. His considerable experience in enterprise software sales provided the perfect foundation for Tope's new venture, yielding enormous success and inspiring many budding Black entrepreneurs along the way.

At eighteen, while studying for a degree and working at a pharmacy, he noticed the cash registers weren't adding up correctly. He decided to create an invention to use optical character recognition to determine which bills and coins were being used in the register. His invention proved successful and became patented. After reading about the founder of Plenty of Fish making nearly $10 million a year for ten hours of work in a *New York Times* piece, his entrepreneurial spirit was fired up. Subsequently, he launched multiple ventures, ranging from a dating website, ProjectorSpot (selling projectors), to YardSteals (a platform for home and yard equipment). His dedication to innovating has propelled him far in his young career as an entrepreneur (Mubarik 2021).

Through his sheer will and commitment to succeed, today thousands of teams across the globe use Calendly to make millions of one-click meetings every week. At the time of writing this book, Calendly has ten million users worldwide, fifty thousand companies using it, and over one hundred partner integrations. The company closed its $350 million series B earlier this year in a funding round led by OpenView. Tope is also the recipient of the 2021 Atlanta Business Chronicle Most Admired CEO Award and 2019 Comparably Best CEOs award.

If there's one characteristic that all successful entrepreneurs share, it's an unshakable sense of determination. Entrepreneurship is not for the faint of heart. It takes grit, tenacity, and a whole lot of hard work. Those who are able to turn their vision into reality are often those who never give up, even when the going gets tough.

In addition to determination, it often requires creativity, risk-taking, and a willingness to learn from mistakes. Being able to pivot when necessary is also key. Many successful businesses have started out as one thing and then morphed into something else entirely based on market demand or other factors. The most important thing is to have a clear vision and the drive to make it happen. With that combination, anything is possible.

THE ONES WHO ARE CRAZY ENOUGH TO THINK THEY CAN CHANGE THE WORLD

So often we hear people say they wish they had followed their childhood dreams. You have known Riddhiman Das from my earlier chapter on personal brand. But there is more than just one thing that makes him so successful.

Das's enthusiasm when speaking about technology is palpable. He lights up while talking, and it's as if he taps into a different energy, using his words to enthusiastically transport the listener back in time—to when he was just a child innocently dreaming of achieving his goals. When asked what sets him apart, he begins by referring to Randy Pausch's famous Carnegie Mellon University lecture about living out childhood dreams: "You are successful if you'd have lived up to what your eight-year-old wanted to do." Das has clearly taken these words to heart and continues to use them as an anchor for motivation throughout his journey as an entrepreneur. His unique approach to success radiates from his eyes from behind his big black spectacles and shines through as he speaks endlessly about technology and life lessons.

He continued to reflect that although he is often blind to his own psychological cues, he has been very fortunate in that since early childhood, he has known what he wanted to do.

"I was probably around five years old when I first learned you could program computers, and I had decided that was what I wanted to do when I grew up. My eight-year-old self would have said that I want to invent new software. My fifteen-year-old self would have said I want to work at the edge of what's possible in technology. And today, I'm not eight, I'm not fifteen, but I'm doing exactly those things. I'm working at the edge of what's possible in software. I have built a career out of that. It's a very specific thing. I never wanted to work on existing software. I'm not a good maintenance programmer or someone who would make incremental improvements to the system."

At Alibaba, he brought biometrics to the world in a way that had never existed before. At TripleBlind, he brought privacy to the world in a way that has never existed before. He has created new possibilities for global access to financial and health services, completely transforming the world of data protection. TripleBlind's revolutionary impact provides people with a level of security they have never experienced before.

"Enabling something that has never been done before gets me excited and energized today, and it is the same thing that got an eight-year-old and a fifteen-year-old in me excited at that time." Fifteen years of professional experience has given him a sharp intuition for rapidly emerging technological fields and which solutions are truly relevant. He recognized the potential to give people control over their privacy and use the TripleBlind platform to achieve secure data sharing, something that was missing from existing solutions at the time. He is quick to add, "But, how does that change the world? What's the outcome of that? TripleBlind has been able to become the world's category leading privacy company. We had an initial vision that played to my strengths, my zones of genius, which is that certain technological approach that was superior to the other solutions out in the field."

"The ones who are crazy enough to think they can change the world are the ones that do," according to Steve Jobs, stands true for entrepreneurship. Everything starts with a dream.

> *An entrepreneur's job is to be obsessive about a problem and be a catalyst to enable a solution.*

Through my work in mentoring and coaching start-ups, I've met a ton of founders in the last three years, and I've learned a few things about how they tick. One interesting trait they've all had in common is *obsession*. And this obsession helps them solve problems. It requires them to dig deeper into the issue, research potential solutions extensively, and pivot if needed, rather than sticking with their solution. They don't want to settle for something that may not be the optimal fix when something better exists. They always remain inquisitive and innovating.

The other role that founders often assume is that of a catalyst, playing a pivotal role in creating change by helping bring these solutions closer to reality. They do this by thinking outside the box, having access to resources that others do not have, and staying informed on potential advancements in the industry.

As is clear in above examples, start-up founders are a rare breed. Key qualities that make them determined to succeed are: being obsessive about a problem; having the drive to beat all odds to convert their vision to reality; being crazy enough to think they can change the world; acting as a catalyst to enable change; and having a tenacity to not break down in the worst of situations.

They have an ability to see opportunity where others see risk and the drive to turn their vision into a reality. They also have in-built resilience against criticisms and doubts from external parties, as they know that these negative voices can easily pull away focus from the ambition if they take root. They recognize them for what they are—nothing more than noise—and stay on course! Most importantly, they are prepared for the roller coaster ride that is start-up life. They know there will be highs and lows, triumphs and defeats. But as long as they learn from their mistakes and keep their eye on the prize, they know they will be successful.

And keeping the prize may also not always mean staying the CEO of the company. Persistence is about being enduring for your idea or vision to live on. There is a very interesting and relevant example I remember from a VC, Robin Klein of LocalGlobe VC.

In one of the guest lectures during the Newton Venture Program, where Robin was a guest speaker, he shared an example that stayed with me. He talked about the first company that LocalGlobe VC backed was the founder who wanted to build sort of the Netflix of Europe. It was called Video Island that later went on and merged with Love Film, and then was acquired by Amazon Music. It was a hugely successful thing. Robin recalled, "The founder got to a certain point with about $12 million in revenue, and he thought he was really not cut out to grow this business any further."

Robin talked about how this founder was very self-aware, referring to when the founder said if they were to make this business reach further heights, they should already get somebody who's run a business of this size and this complexity. Robin added, "We appointed a chief executive officer who took it all the way to Amazon. But the founder himself remained on the board. What he really cared about was that the company lived." Robin gave a great analogy with reference to this example: "Companies are like the lives of people. They evolve and they change. We have seen that with Google, and we have seen that with Microsoft."

David Hornik talked about the importance of also understanding what is knowable and doing everything in your power to know what is knowable. I would add my own bits to David and Robin's views: Entrepreneurs should not shy away from bringing in people who are more skilled than they are. We have also seen that with Babu, when he merged his business Envestnet when the going got tough, and it turned out to be a great collaboration.

It takes a great deal of determination, ambition, and focus on the part of founders to open their projects up to others. Investors don't require that a founder knows everything but rather they may know a lot about a little. They should have the capacity to learn, the willingness to listen, and the leadership skills to create a team to fill in the gaps. It's perfectly fine to be aware of your weaknesses; having the knowledge of what you don't know is a strength. At the end of the day, nobody has all the answers. It's up to the founder to determine how they'll go about addressing their knowledge gaps rather than trying to do it all themselves or throwing in the towel.

If you're an entrepreneur reading this and feeling down about the obstacles you're facing, remember that progress isn't always accomplished through big wins. There's beauty to be found in the small successes along your journey. Each step forward is an important one and shouldn't be overlooked. When you feel stuck, focus on the progress you've already made and celebrate the wins, no matter how minor! Appreciating yourself for what you are accomplishing gives a much-needed morale boost that encourages you to continue along the path of success. As you work toward larger goals, use fear as a tool. It's a sign that this goal is meaningful enough for you to take risks. In order to stay determined, focus on why you're doing this. Your goals can serve as fuel when motivation wavers.

CHAPTER 8

MAKE YOUR IDEAS STICK: START A MOVEMENT

MYTH: ISN'T IT NATURAL—AND INEVITABLE— THAT ENTREPRENEURS WHO WORK HARDER AND HAVE GREAT IDEAS GO FURTHER?

Let me start by asking you a question. Have you ever heard someone having just an idea, or a start-up in initial stages, that seemed like an amazing solution to a big problem, and you thought this would be such a stellar business? Even without seeing you right now, I know you are nodding as you are reading. And that's because this happens regularly to all of us.

Great ideas feel exciting. They are inspiring! You just know when someone is on to something.

Now think of the times it has happened when one of those great ideas were actually converted to a business—and a successful one at that. I am certain you are scrambling in your head to look for examples, and there would be only a few common ones that must be coming to your mind— Airbnb, Uber, Facebook, Etsy, Lego... And that makes sense! Because, actually, the best ideas are definitely not always the ones that stick or take off.

In fact, the journey of putting great ideas into action is often a very long one—and can feel really hard for entrepreneurs.

If you are a founder, reading this book, you might be juggling to find exact these answers right now. "How do I create the next disruption?"

All the fans of business model innovation and product market fit, (desirability, viability, feasibility; addressing the customer pain point; prototyping and testing), I hear you. I know the answers running in your head. I am coaching several start-ups daily on how to come up with innovation, design for disruption, and prepare for the next big thing. But this book is not about how to make innovation happen or how to make that sell. It is about how to make the solution reach the people who need it to be solved.

It's not always headline-grabbing innovation that makes disruption, but rather its capacity to ascertain possibilities in what is already in existence, learning from earlier mistakes of other founders who built something similar, and building something extraordinary with dedication and help of communities that will ultimately have the same effect.

The main problem with amazing start-up ideas isn't necessarily coming up with something truly innovative (although that is hard enough). In my experience working with many different entrepreneurs, I've noticed the difficulty lies in conveying the message to investors, stakeholders, partners, consumers, and any other influencers. This is often the curse of knowledge: The person sharing the idea has all sorts of insider information that others don't.

The reason an idea does not reach the intended audience is because the person sharing the idea has all sorts of information that others don't. They have already framed the problem and understood its relevance, but the listener does not yet have the same context, leaving them unable to appreciate the magnitude of its importance and gain the necessary traction.

Making great ideas stick and spread is actually *less* unicorn and *more* in our individual power than many of us think.

The key here, though, is knowing how to influence this, and where to start.

Below are the six elements to achieving great idea adoption—and what is in our own power to make sure this happens:

1. A DESIRED FUTURE.

You must be familiar with this one. This is the hunger, the drive, and the vision that a founder brings to the table.

Going back to the question I asked you at the start of this chapter, about how many of the great ideas you've heard ever get past the "wouldn't it be nice" phase? It starts here, with this moment. Does the founder envision and desire a future for this idea—one that they hold with unwavering commitment?

Of course, it is important to see how ambitious they really are in fulfilling their purpose, but what is even more important is how ambitious the purpose itself is.

As Babu Sivadasan spoke, his voice was filled with pride. "We were competing against each other tooth and nail, but when we came together it was very complementary skills, and that really enabled us to propel ourselves. We were unstoppable!" His eyes sparkled with an intensity as he recounted the story. "For the next fourteen years, we became the largest wealth management technology company in the world. So, we built, we went public in 2010, we worked with every leading financial organization." He added with a satisfied smile, "It turned out pretty well. We defined wealth management, a gold standard with a leading cloud-based platform."

As he spoke, his eyes gleamed with pride as he remembered the journey that had led to Envestnet's landmark merger. He recalled his early ambition to revolutionize the wealth management segment and his unwavering commitment to spend two decades of his life working to create this change. "I had people from my hometown who believed in me and the product," he said with a hint of nostalgia in his voice. He went on to tell the story of how he had to convince skeptical colleagues to take stock instead of cash for salaries, an undertaking which initially seemed daunting. His recall of this moment was one of admiration and appreciation, as in hindsight, they all realized the great value of this mission.

He reflected on the tumultuous time. "It was a crowded field at that time. But we were having some early success." He described how they had to scramble for capital, even though they were trying to revolutionize the financial industry. "No VCs would invest in us. The financial technology industry was relatively new."

He talked about how they struggled and then eventually merged with their biggest competitor. "I had to do that. I remember making salvages, extra personal checks for my team in India, because you let people down who initially believed in you." Eventually, that merger was very complementary.

Babu's story is one of ambition, of a desired future envisioned by an idea holder who refused to relent in the face of adversity. With an unshakeable drive to see his vision realized, Babu poured every ounce of his being into making it happen. His passion was palpable, and his unwavering commitment to his cause inspired those around him.

Babu is on another mission now to disrupt the way companies automate their complicated business operations. Their app-based, cognitive automation platform gives its business users the opportunity to experiment with developing cutting-edge technologies. This platform features various capabilities, from natural language processing and intelligent document processing to robotic process automation and competitive low code/no code development. Furthermore, their platform is the only one that can recognize mistakes and disparities in documents like loans, invoices, and claims, then fix them with its self-learning functionality.

As we see in this example of Babu, hunger and drive are key to making great ideas come to life, but the unwavering commitment to stay the course and have faith in the desired future others don't yet see is important.

Chris Smith, of Playfair Capital, leaned back in his chair and thoughtfully shared his insights on the subject of how investors evaluate projects. "There's something special that happens when an entrepreneur describes their concept and you just know. You can feel it." His eyes lit up as he continued. "What we're really looking at is the drive of the founder; the passion and purpose behind their mission. If a founder is motivated, their enthusiasm is naturally infectious."

He went on to explain the intriguing question that each partner must answer when evaluating projects: "If given the opportunity, would you work for this founder?" He chuckled and said, "It may sound like a fun game, but it reveals how serious we are about each venture. It speaks to our level of conviction in both the vision and the person behind it."

Tristan Walker talks about the motivation and values held by the idea holder. "So these founders bring a natural energy and enthusiasm and authenticity that makes people want to work with them, as opposed to people who are driven by building something because it's fashionable or because they want to make a ton of money" (James 2023). He says he often gets people who are inspired by his success, asking him if they should become a founder.

His face softened into a thoughtful expression as he spoke. "The answer should always be met with a question as well. Are you so passionate about what you're building that you can't sleep? That motivation really plays a role. And then think in terms of getting people to join you. You need to bring them in. Initial days of start-up, you're building a tribe, or like a band of people who are completely set on the same mission. Everyone needs to believe in your vision. And if the vision is clear, building a brand is really easy, and the adoption and traction just happens."

2. PAINTING THE VISION THROUGH MEANINGFUL STORIES OF CHANGE.

The key to making an idea memorable is to tell it as a story. Stories encourage the listener to live the experience and emotionally connect with the audience. Storytelling is an age-old tradition, providing us with many fundamental tools for making sense of our ideas in the minds of those we seek to gain support from.

Of course, the challenging part is constructing an effective story. Think of campaigns that have changed the way you think; maybe success stories you have read about that have excited you about an organization or inspired you to purchase from them. This sharing is critical in the beginning of an idea to attach the kind of emotion and enthusiasm that helps ideas gain momentum.

Nike is a brand that does this well, as is Volkswagen. And remember Marlboro Man? This is a great example of a brand painting a vision of a freedom lifestyle. Although it's now wildly outdated—for many years, people came to associate freedom with smoking due to the way the brand told the story. Through clever "painting the vision," Marlboro managed to tap into the self-image people had of themselves and created brand loyalty through connecting the individual not just with a product, but also the lifestyle they imagine themselves to have.

And if you see closely, none of these brands talk about the product itself. Their story is about the aspirations they fulfill. Nike is arguably the best example of this with its thirty-year-old "Just do it" slogan. These are stories of ideas created that have become more important than the product itself, creating wealth and building fortunes.

Most founders think this is part of marketing and branding. They are of the opinion that in the early stages, you need to build traction, not a brand or marketing. But that is exactly my point. Building a brand for your product (rather the aspiration you want to solve for) and telling its story can actually get you that early traction.

Consumers tend to focus more on the outcomes of their purchasing decisions rather than the decision itself. To illustrate this point, let me use the example of gym memberships. This kind of purchase appeals to people because it promises a more fit body in the end. This ultimate goal motivates people to buy the *goal*, not the membership itself.

When founders are building products and their pitch decks, they are only thinking of features, or product need in tangible terms. They are often overlooking the emotional, intangible, and aspirational need of the product, which can often be the biggest factor in achieving idea adoption. The stories on your pitch deck to investors, or on traction building promotions, or the first communities you tap into, should focus on that end goal of the consumer, not the product itself.

Also, when you are building your Minimum Viable Product (MVP) for testing, don't just do the experiment for the product prototype, do it also for the desire and aspiration or the vision for that product. This helps you in two ways: one, if your idea speaks to people on an emotional and aspirational level, you can do pivots and experiment within a branded community that would still be a fan of your vision; and two, you build your brand following way earlier than most competitors, hence your idea would gain traction faster than any of the other similar product in the market. The possible third benefit is that you could launch testing even before your MVP is launched, like testing the vision before testing the product.

For ideas to reach a tipping point in adoption, you need to start sharing the story much earlier than you think. It comes before the product is even conceived. Because let's face it—when you have a great story there is no obstacle too large to overcome! You just need to be creative and tell a story about something your product can enable, but that hasn't happened yet.

Traction: Let's look this in perspective. What data can be leveraged in early stages of an idea to add persuasion? The idea is to bring statistics compelling to take action:

- How many people may have the aspiration you want to solve for, and what is the source of their aspiration?
- Or what external story or idea is wildly different from yours but is known to people, which can powerfully engage them?
- Or start with "imagine if more people did that" stories and surveys.

David Hornik stared intently at me, his eyebrows furrowed together in concentration. He cleared his throat and said in a deep, authoritative voice, "When it comes to venture capitalists evaluating a start-up, traction is key. But what does traction really mean?" He paused before he answered. "To put it simply, it's evidence that an idea is feasible, innovative, and worth investing in."

David's question captures the essence of what a potential investor wants to find out: Is there any concrete proof that makes this worth backing—traction or evidence? David talks about how to think about traction and building evidence in terms of metrics you could collect. Either you are on Facebook, and you had thousands of people who are visiting your company's account two hours a day—that is a pretty good indicator, because it shows this is something people care about. He added, "Or you have sold something to a big company for $50,000. And then six months later, they pay you another $50,000 because they want more of it."

He elaborated there are all sorts of ways to figure out if you are really solving a problem anyone cares about. And if you are solving it in a smart and thoughtful way, it makes people engage. That is yet another important piece.

Chris Smith gave a very interesting example of how founders have often read on Twitter or in press that XYZ raised twenty million off the back of a pitch deck. He said, "I think that's just a horrible misrepresentation of what founders actually need to do to raise money in 99 percent of cases." He said founders have lots of resources. They can do friends and family rounds, or bootstrap, but they should have built an MVP and find out if their product and story has a market. He added an example, "We have one company where they surveyed over two hundred businesses to figure out if the software they were building would make that business's life easier. This is a demonstration of productivity at an early stage."

He said among investors, there is also this notion, "If companies start fast, they can continue moving quickly. And that's important to get to venture scale. But companies that start slow, it's really hard, if not impossible, to speed them up. Because it's baked into your culture and baked into your DNA as a company. So we really expect founders, even with limited means, to have done as much as they can to de-risk the investment and prove and bring a story of traction."

Dan Matthies says the most important thing he looks at in a pitch is if the founder clearly stated what problem they're going to solve and how they're going to solve it differently. And also, why people are going to embrace their solution and not others. He had an interesting observation here as he said, "People who speak with examples and stories are always more convincing because they can say, 'Here's the data,' and that makes it tangible." He paused and said, "That speaks more volumes."

Next time you think about your product, think about what aspirations it would fulfill. And for the presentations, ditch your slides and go for stories.

- **Story of the product (emotion behind the purchase):** It could be either where it came from and why it is needed, or it could also be a story of the aspiration or desired future of your customer.

- **Story of the founder and team:** You need to prove to investors your team can execute on the idea—build a world-class product and sell it to millions of people.

That doesn't come just with the years of experience in a certain job. You want to focus on what you learned on that job and how you are integrating that in building your product, or what your background is that makes you uniquely positioned to solve for that problem.

- **Story of traction:** Here, metrics and evidence are projected in data and numbers, but also it needs to be a story of how many lives you are touching, improving, and helping; how they feel after they use your product, how many emotions or aspirations has your product fulfilled. Numbers can tell a story too.

- **Evidence of traction:** If you already started selling, collect your sales data. If not, seek out methods for you to do a pre-sales test. This may include having people sign up for an email list, taking pre-orders, or any other ways you can measure customers' interest in your product. Afterward, look at your metrics such as conversion rates to demonstrate how there is likely to be a steady amount of buyers.

3. ENGAGE YOUR CUSTOMERS IN BUILDING YOUR BRAND.

This point has to do with what's commonly known as the "Ikea effect." A 2011 study explains why people place higher value on things they helped to build or create. It is described as a cognitive bias that occurs when we put effort into acquiring a product, or help in building or shaping it, and hence tend to overvalue things we are involved in making (Norton, Mochon, and Ariely 2011).

Think LEGO. It continues to grow and thrive even in the age of too much screen time—and it's likely that customer engagement plays a big role here. Customers love to have a say in the development of the products they enjoy, and the LEGO Ideas community gives its customers that power.

"In 2008, LEGO launched the LEGO Ideas platform, allowing fans to submit new concepts for LEGO sets. Proposals are voted on by other fans, and top vote-getters are reviewed by LEGO staff. Chosen ideas are turned into sets for sale. The fan designer receives 1 percent of the royalties. This community has grown to over a million users, more than 26,000 product ideas have been submitted, and twenty-eight sets produced. Through LEGO Ideas, the eighty-seven-year-old company successfully transitioned from simply building for customers to building with an engaged community" (Richardson, Kevin, and Sotto 2020).

Twitch and Instagram have both been incredibly successful in part due to their vibrant communities. They have both been purchased by public parent companies (Amazon and Facebook, respectively). But they've taken remarkably different paths with their community investments. Instagram was once a community-building darling. As cofounder Kevin Systrom explained, "Anyone can create a photo-sharing app; not everyone can create a community. If you can protect that asset—if you can help nurture and grow it—and your product doesn't suck, you have created something much more valuable than a great product with a terrible community" (Richardson, Kevin, and Sotto 2020).

Start-up pride themselves on their ability to be customer focused, understand the experiences and insights of the marketplace, and use these observations and ideas to improve their products later. However, just think of how much more successful your start-up could be if you tapped into the valuable knowledge of the people who use your existing (or soon-to-be existing) products and let them help you with your research and development initiatives?

4. STRUCTURAL HOLES: FILLING IN THE GAPS BENEFITS YOU AND THE COMMUNITIES.

The concept of structural holes that we coach on as part of Professor Jeffrey Pfeffer's class, "Building Power to LEAD" at Stanford Graduate School of Business have inspired me. I am an executive coach in the online version of the class with Jeff. I have worked with hundreds of global executives through the Stanford LEAD program, where I see them make use of this and many other principles and create an outsized impact on their personal development while benefiting the communities they are part of.

Structural holes are a concept from social network research. It refers to a "space" between contacts in a person's network. It means these contacts do not inter-act closely (though they may be aware of one another).

There is a gap between two individuals or communities with complementary resources or information. And the theory demonstrates that users occupying the bridging positions between different communities have advantages (Burt 1992).

Having experienced the diversity and generosity of the Stanford GSB LEAD alum community first-hand, I was dismayed with the lack of formal structures and resources to encourage creativity and spark innovation within the network, apart from the formal Stanford program courses. In 2020, I cofounded LISA (a volunteer program)—Stanford GSB LEAD Incubator and Start-up Accelerator—with Edward Mundt and a few others in an effort to fill that gap.

With the help of some of the sharpest minds in the community, we built a ten-week-long incubation program that serves to foster start-up ideas from over five thousand global alums of Stanford LEAD. This has been my mini-entrepreneurial stint, which has been a joy to be part of. I am immensely proud of our impact in inspiring and equipping leaders to keep networking beyond the program while also helping to build start-up ventures within the community.

Through LISA, we masterminded an innovative and flourishing ecosystem to support the growth of start-up founders. We attracted the attention of hundreds of global community members and engaged them through design facilitation, mentorship, and various expert-led workshops. With the help of faculty and staff, we utilized

Stanford's entrepreneurship curriculum to expand LISA's vision. So far, we have incubated over 150 ideas spread over five cohorts, with founders represented in more than thirty-six countries, and affected change in an ecosystem ripe for entrepreneurship.

In building LISA, we applied the structural holes theory by bridging two communities that were existent but dormant. We built the bridge between founders and the expertise in the community. Here, we considered the strategy that generates groups, structures, events, or activities with some institutional permanence, creates recurring visibility and access—and potentially grows in value over time.

While building LISA and its community, we did not try to build everything on our own. In fact, we got a community involved as executive team members, empowered them to contribute, and let them lead with our vision! This was because we wanted to foster the collective intelligence of people. (If you are in innovation, you know how valuable this can be.) This also enabled us to get helping hands to build our vision into a larger-than-life project, which could only scale if it did not remain in a few hands as initial founders.

We crafted the purpose and vision people wanted to be part of and who could also derive value from it by associating with it. We enabled a platform, community, and events—something tangible to which they could contribute. Our fundamental reason for success was that we always remembered to raise people and give them credit for what they have been helping us build, and we always gave them space to shine out. Hence, the overall mission multiplied, and the impact was multifold. Today, LISA is synonymous with Stanford LEAD online program for people within the LEAD alumni community, and we, as founders and all team members working with it, have brand equity built on this initiative. Did the idea become sticky? Well, yes!

While navigating, building, scaling, and continuing the momentum of the LISA community, Edward and I had to transition from being a founder of an accelerator to acting like a CEO and captain of the ship. It changed our perspective on entrepreneurship from starting this initiative with a small team. It meant resilience when few of the early cofounders parted ways, with just the two of us now left as co-founders.

Attracting talent and teams to join as helping hands, building relationships with Stanford staff to enable faculty-designed curriculum, constantly investing in LISA brand building through various promotional and founder events, getting VCs to start associating with us for panel discussions and pitch fests, getting advisors and mentors to work with our recruited founders—all this required building power and influence and embracing a set of skills that we may not have started out with.

We needed to quickly start building networks and lasting relationships, inspiring people to take action, asking for what we wanted, being determined and focused on what we needed, and carving a creative way out to succeed.

5. LEAN INTO COLLECTIVE INTELLIGENCE OF A COMMUNITY AND EMPOWER THEM TO SELF-MOBILIZE.

The fifth way that great ideas get adopted is by leaning into the collective intelligence of a community. Through pooled knowledge and open collaboration, larger than life projects can materialize.

Etsy has an important lesson for entrepreneurs here. It's essential to have advocates who believe in your cause and are willing to help you move your mission forward. Building a community of passionate people around your project is one of the most important factors for success. Not only can they become customers and collaborators, but they can help build momentum, boost morale, and bring visibility to you or your product. When creating a business or pursuing a new idea, having proponents who are dedicated to seeing it succeed gives it power and potential that would otherwise be missing.

In the 1980s, Harley-Davidson faced a difficult task of rebranding and reviving their company. This presents an interesting example for start-up companies when they consider pivoting their strategy to appeal to customers. Harley-Davidson's strategy included building a strong community that would foster loyalty and propel growth, with the eventual goal of becoming a lifestyle brand.

Harley-Davidson used communities to build their product following, promoting a sense of connection between fans. This iconic brand has been making motorcycles for over a century and has created both official and unofficial rider clubs across the world. To bring their followers together, they established the Harley Owners Club, which has since become one of the most well-known motorcycling communities on the internet.

The Harley Owners Club encourages its enthusiasts to identify with the brand and provides them with access to exclusive offers and benefits. For example, members can attend official events, join local chapters, and receive added services such as insurance and roadside assistance. These efforts foster customer loyalty and enable riders to get more out of their experience with Harley-Davidson.

You need to build your village. You can't be successful on your own, which is especially true for a lot of Networking organizations and platform-based communities and businesses that have a common purpose, goal, or pain point.

"Think of community-building as progressive acts of collaboration that demand trust from the company or original leader. Consider TED's decision to invest in TEDx. Founded as an invitation-only conference in 1984, TED made a bold decision to introduce TEDx in 2009, empowering volunteers to independently organize TED-style conferences in their own cities. By doing so, they allowed massive numbers of attendees to participate, including those who could never afford the central TED conference's elite price tag" (Richardson, Kevin, and Sotto 2020).

An example is Deepa Purushothaman, a former senior executive at Deloitte, who wanted to see more women of color in leadership roles. She organized a series of twelve dinners of women of color in order for them to connect and grow. However, she knew she couldn't do this quickly and do it well without a community. She quickly empowered the initial leaders to extend their reach into new areas, allowing her idea to gain momentum and spread like wildfire. Quickly, her organization, nFormation, grew from a dinner of twelve into meetups, networking, information exchange, and content for thousands of women of color all over the world.

Leveraging community is a crucial way for many ideas to gain not only adoption but also momentum.

Deepa recalled how she took a leap of faith and quit her job. "I did not leave Deloitte knowing exactly what I was going to do next. I left in the early stages of COVID-19, before we called it the great resignation. My company nFormation came out of the dinners that we did, where I was trying to figure out what I wanted to do next. I initially started talking to women of color one on one. Those eventually turned into about a dozen dinners across the country, where I ended up meeting three hundred women of color. I did not think that was going to be a business. I was just trying to figure out, What is it that I want to do? I didn't even know how to break out of the toy bubble. All I knew was I wanted to do something in DEI (diversity, equity, and inclusion) space. So I was really listening for those kinds of conversations."

Her face lit up as she added, "Until a CFO of a public company said I sit in the seat of power, and I don't feel

powerful. And that became really fascinating to me."
This piqued her interest. She did twelve of those dinners across the US with her partner and coach at the
time. They were just calling people they didn't know,
announcing they were going to be in New York (or the
other cities), asking friends, or reaching out on LinkedIn.
It was very unplanned and more like networking. Those
dinners were magical for the women. They would finish
each other's sentences. They didn't have other relationships with senior women, since they were the first, the
few, and the only in those positions of power and very
isolated in the spaces they operated in. All they wanted
was to be in a community.

6. CREATE INSTITUTIONS OF PERMANENCE THROUGH ALLYSHIP; BUILD A TEAM OF LIKE-MINDED ALLIES.

Creating permanent systems around allyship is the final
puzzle piece I uncovered in my research on entrepreneurship and the key element in the "stickiness" that great
ideas needed in order to have staying power. Going at
it alone as an entrepreneur can be a great way to build
ideas and make them a reality, but having the help and
support of a community can accelerate this process expo-
nentially. When various stakeholders come together to
achieve something big, they are able to create a momentum for the idea and add resources to fuel it that may not
be available to one person.

This is a place where many of us here today have the opportunity to step in and really influence idea adoption. Let me share an example of Girls Who Code, and its founder, Reshma Saujani. Reshma's idea was "Let's get more girls into coding"—and for this to gain traction, it needed allied power. To do this, Reshma and her team connected with leaders of companies, government, special interest organizations—everyone they felt could advance their idea and would gain from getting invested in their idea through networks other than their own. This allied power, fueled by believers in the idea, pushed forward the organization in a way that institutional traditional power could not.

Reshma's team also created permanence for her idea through allyship. By creating programs, internships, mentorships, and other initiatives that are driven by allies, their team essentially institutionalized Girls Who Code. They created a movement and gave it staying power.

I find allyship to be such an important part of increasing diversity in the entrepreneurship ecosystem, not just getting ideas adopted, that I have the whole next chapter dedicated to it. You will learn more about Reshma's motivations behind Girls Who Code and how she got started.

Something similar is what Swapna Gupta of AVANA Capital talked about that is in the power of venture capitalists to create. What Swapna created is also what Chris had done at Playfair Capital with Women Founders Hour that he talked about in one of the previous chapters when he brought together twelve investors in the beginning for the first event. Now it has scaled to hundreds of investors and founders taking part in this initiative globally. They are creating a movement.

Swapna said, "At Qualcomm Ventures, one of the things I was continuously seeing, as we were doing late-stage investments, is that more often than not, I would see male founders getting supported by us. I was just appalled at why I'm not seeing enough women founders." So, she started this program called Qualcomm Women Entrepreneur, which is now in the third year running successfully after she left the organization. The idea was to get fifteen women entrepreneurs every year in very early-stage ideas and coach them. With that initiative, Swapna wanted to equip them to prepare for funding in series A and improve the funnel. She engaged stakeholders from within Qualcomm as allies in this idea. As it became a shared goal, it did not just get adopted, it stuck.

So as you can see, these six elements are key in determining whether a great idea gets adopted *and* can stick:

1. **A desired future.**
2. **Painting the vision through meaningful stories of change.**
3. **Engage your customers in building your brand.**
4. **Structural holes: Filling in the gaps benefits you and the communities.**
5. **Lean into collective intelligence of a community and empower them to self-mobilize.**
6. **Create institutions of permanence through allyship; build a team of like-minded allies.**

You might want to apply the idea of a social tipping point when you are thinking of idea adoption or traction to gain momentum on what you are building. If there is just one thing you want to take away from this chapter, an easy conclusion to draw is:

An idea sticks and takes-off when it becomes a movement.

CHAPTER 9

POLISH EXECUTIVE PRESENCE: NO ONE INVESTS IN YOUR IMPOSTER SYNDROME

"Far too often, executives fail to align their physical energy with what they want to achieve. When we talk about energy, we mean both the superficial layer- how you look- and the vibe you give off-the mood and tone you convey. How you appear to others matters as much as what you say."

—AMY JEN SU

"It is executive presence—and no man or woman attains a top job, lands an extraordinary deal, or develops a significant following without this heady combination of confidence, poise, and authenticity that convinces the rest of us we're in the presence of someone who's the real deal. It's an amalgam of qualities that telegraphs that you are in charge or deserve to be."

—SYLVIA ANN HEWLETT

"You know my height is five feet and one inch, but I always say five feet and four inches with the heels, and that's what makes a great deal of difference!" said Maria Castellon. Her bright red shirt was radiating her confidence while her posture showed she had worked a lot on having that executive poise. She is a reflection of what intentional practice and the right attitude can do. She perfectly embodied how practice can transform one into a leader of influence in any situation. She hit the nail on the head through her words that even seemingly small adjustments can make a big impact.

Maria and I shared a knowing smile as she quipped about her height. We knew too well the unfairness of the bias that taller people tend to have more authority, status, and prestige. Research has even backed up this notion in studies such as "The Height Leadership Advantage in Men and Women: Testing Evolutionary Psychology Predictions about the Perception of Tall Leaders" (Blaker et al. 2013). Despite often being at a disadvantage in this regard, we both cherish our ability to level the playing field by beating the biases we are often faced with.

I have myself been an underdog who faced huge obstacles in my attempt to assume the positions I wanted. I often felt like an outsider because of my gender, age, and ethnicity. I grew up in India but moved to Europe for work at the age of twenty-five. Despite this, one thing that kept me going was my determination to prove everyone wrong and level the playing field without the aid of any special privilege. The only way possible was by working on and developing my executive presence.

I saw a lot of commonalities between me and Maria. We both strived for greatness, refusing to let anyone's preconceived ideas take away from our ambition, and it has been incredibly rewarding. Knowing our strength of mind and perseverance can triumph over prejudice gives us immense satisfaction.

Nearly thirty years ago, when Maria Castellon arrived in Silicon Valley from Guadalajara, Mexico, she had only a high school education and had yet to learn English. Now, she is the CEO of Bench-Tek Solutions, a family-owned, $10 million firm that designs and manufactures workbenches and laboratory stations for use in production and cleanroom environments. She serves major tech giants Apple, Google, PG&E, Nvidia, Sandia Labs, and Tesla among its client roster.

Maria Castellon's story is one of grit and determination. She immigrated to the United States from Mexico in pursuit of a college education and ended up taking a job as a janitor at IBM. Little did she know she would be the founder of Bench-Tek solutions—an incredible success story! Her Silicon Valley manufacturing facility specializes in custom design and manufacturing of workbenches, carts, racks, and modular workstations to meet the needs of companies in any industry requiring secure storage—including manufacturing, laboratories, cleanrooms, tech spaces, R&D facilities, industrial plants, automotive applications, and environments requiring

ESD-safe standards. With a global presence across four continents and six countries, Maria has proven that hard work really does pay off!

You might be wondering how being tall would have anything to do with being perceived as a more capable leader. As per the study mentioned above, one possible explanation from an evolutionary standpoint is that in the animal kingdom, larger individuals who do battle often fare better than smaller ones, conferring upon them a degree of power and dominance. We can observe this same tendency in humans: tall people may subconsciously appear more powerful and intelligent to onlookers, granting them respect and the perception they are better suited for leadership positions. Tallness confers an advantage in terms of executive presence, one of the many facets of one's gravitas.

Executive presence is not simply a matter of height. Rather, it is a combination of factors, including your posture, your body language, how you dress, how you sit, what words you use, the pauses you take when you talk, and even your vocal tone. The executive presence is about the signal of your preparedness; how decisive and assertive you come across. Executive presence essentially refers to the ability to project confidence and authority through your words and actions.

Maria worked on all these areas to be taken seriously as a petite Latina woman when she started out her journey as an entrepreneur. Her story reminded me of my own journey as I landed in Germany from India fifteen years back. Maria talked about not only the biases, but also her self-imposed limitations she faced at that time. "My hair was dark when I started, and I looked very young for my age. I had to put my hair up to look more professional."

She added, "Women in cultural minorities are taught to be compliant. It's hard for us to say no. I wanted to please everybody. I wanted to bend backward to get an order. A lot had to do with my fear to speak more assertively, to communicate to my clients as to why I needed to sell my product at that price that it deserved."

One of the first things she decided to change about herself was her executive presence. To do this, she realized it was time to overcome her self-limiting beliefs, fears, and timidness that had been holding her back from achieving the success and recognition she desired. She made an effort to become more assertive, charismatic, and confident in her approach while also changing her mindset. To get on the right path, she sought advice through formal mentorships, coaching programs, and training sessions to help new skills become second nature.

As she drove between countless cities—Santa Clara, Sacramento, and San Francisco—she used her car as her personal library. With the entire library of Tony Robbins's work, a customer generously gifted her, she was able to use those quiet moments in between stops for personal development. "It was a lot of those quiet moments that I have had in my car listening to Robbins, and I needed it because I had a lot of blocks in my mind and in my own thinking." It was in that car that Maria's next chapter began, evolving into someone who continues to inspire many today.

She further worked on her styling. "I was very fortunate with my ex-boss and always thanked him. He mentored me on how to dress with tailor suits and my looks so I can feel confident in my persona." With unique and oftentimes racialized perceptions of what is deemed as "professional," some individuals may feel they need to curate their entire look to appear as if they belong or are capable and worthy of certain roles. This was certainly not left unexplored by Maria—realizing the need to "dress two levels up" in order to achieve better results—but it is often a challenge felt by many minority women.

Maria was no stranger to judgment based on her appearance and personality and the fear that these could impact how much her clients, partners, and investors valued her business and her capability to be a successful entrepreneur. She talked about the biases she faced when she started her business and before she invested on the way she looks, acts, and shows up. "I would have my little suitcase, cold calling, walking into companies, and people didn't even wait to hear what I had to say before they said, 'We're not hiring.'"

Maria is proof that working on your self-limiting beliefs and actions, and strategically working at beating the bias, can help you overcome any societal stereotypes and stigma that threaten to hold you back. She had been clearly labeled, judged, and underestimated.

The path that led to Maria's phenomenal success is equally extraordinary. She had been going from job to job before landing a position as a receptionist in a manufacturing firm. Maria's dedication caught the attention of her boss, Tom Clark, and he quickly began mentoring her. He encouraged her to start taking businesses classes. Over the next decade, Maria built her business acumen.

Today, Maria is a renowned name in Silicon Valley circles, which she attributes to her work on herself and her relentless networking skills, some of which I talk about in the networking chapter. She started with $20,000 in savings. Today, Bench-Tek own three buildings in Santa Clara, which collectively take up twenty thousand square feet. She started with three employees and is now up to eighteen, 70 percent of whom are Latinx, and currently doing $10 million in revenue as of June 2022. And she's working on scaling her business further, having gone through the Stanford Latino Entrepreneur Initiative. Maria's company is also part of Apple's first class of Black- and Brown-owned businesses on the cutting edge of green technology and clean energy, an initiative unveiled in august 2021.

PROJECTING CONFIDENCE CAN BE KEY TO BUSINESS

The start-up phase of a business is when the company is looking for their footing. This is when a founder's executive presence matters the most. In order to develop an effective start-up, the founder must be able to articulate the company's vision and give clear instructions to the team. And it starts right from the stage you start pitching to the investors.

Influential decision-makers want to know how you think, whether your ideas make sense, whether you should be trusted, and whether you have the confidence to pull it all off. Too often, start-up founders focus exclusively on the technical aspects of their pitch, forgetting that how they show up is just as important.

Projecting confidence can be key to business success from the moment you start pitching your idea. It is more than just speaking with authority, making eye contact, and using gestures. You must also have a positive attitude, radiating competence and self-assurance. With this type of aura, potential investors are more likely to back your start-up. It can help them see you as an able leader and give them faith in the success of their investment. When attempting to get funding or support for a project or endeavor, confidence may play a great role in determining its success.

A CRITICAL PIECE OF THE PUZZLE IS HOW YOU LOOK

A groundbreaking study from 2012 cosponsored by *Marie Claire*, American Express, and Goldman Sachs had a similar conclusion: "You'll be judged on at least seventeen different criteria (above and beyond your actual work performance), from seemingly insignificant details like hairstyle and tone of voice to sweeping leadership qualities like vision and decisiveness." So what does that mean for you, as a talented up-and-coming start-up founder? Sylvia Ann Hewlett, an author, economist, and entrepreneur, explains all the not-so-obvious skills you'll need in your arsenal to ensure you get everything you're working so hard for (Claire 2012).

Dr. Hewlett is a celebrated speaker. She has presented at Davos and at the Mobile World Congress, keynoted the *Financial Times* conference on "Women at the Top," and spoken at the White House. She is also a *Glamour* magazine "Woman of the Year," has been interviewed on *60 Minutes*, *Panorama*, *Oprah*, *Morning Joe*, and *PBS Newshour*. Her writings have appeared in the *New York Times*, *Financial Times*, and *Vogue*.

Executive presence is an important attribute needed to move up the ranks in the business world. Sylvia explains that regardless of the work culture a person is involved in (whether Silicon Valley or Wall Street), everyone needs to excel in three pillars to effectively be seen as a deserving future leader: how you look, speak, and behave. Nailing all three things makes you a contender.

"A critical piece of the puzzle is how you look, because it's the first filter. If you show up without makeup or looking sloppy, no matter how impressive your ideas are, no one is going to pay attention to you. People take you more seriously if you look polished." She also talks about six elements of gravitas critical to leadership: grace under fire; decisiveness; emotional intelligence and the ability to read a room; integrity and authentic persona; a vision that inspires others; and a stellar reputation (Hewlett 2014).

Though it is a hard truth, there are biases to which many of us may not be the best equipped to fight against. This can be especially true when those biases come from backgrounds where we do not have enough role models to emulate or look up to. But having knowledge of how certain elements work allow us to battle these biases better than if we were unaware. Through gaining knowledge of certain powerful triggers, such as body language and presentation, we can strengthen our positions and exceed any unfavorable circumstances based on prejudices.

If founders know what works in terms of appearance and body language, they can overcome these obstacles. For example, research has shown that wearing dark colors and maintaining good posture can convey authority and power. By understanding the science of executive presence, start-up founders can give themselves a much-needed boost in the business world.

One area that almost no one ever prepares for if you want to be seen as a leader is to demonstrate vocal executive presence. If you're a start-up founder, you know that pitching is a crucial part of your job. But in the midst of a high-pressure situation, it can be easy to let your nerves get the best of you. While you can't change the voice you were born with, you can control how you use it.

Speaking slowly and deliberately will help you project confidence, while maintaining eye contact and using open body language will make you appear approachable and trustworthy. You have to be able to pitch with confidence and authority and answer tough questions quickly and decisively. The way you conduct yourself when the pressure is on can have an impact on how others will perceive you as someone who could essentially take the role of leading a company, not just executing an idea.

WANT TO SOUND LIKE A LEADER? START BY SAYING YOUR NAME RIGHT

One of the resources I also highly recommend is diving deeper into Dr. Laura Sicola's principles on how to authentically master the three Cs of "vocal executive presence": command the room, connect with the audience, and close the deal. She is a leadership communication and influence expert, speaker, and author of *Speaking to Influence: Mastering Your Leadership Voice*.

Laura is known for her coaching that turns executives into confident, inspiring leaders, whether on stage or on camera. I have personally tried some of her techniques, which help tremendously when getting ready for an important presentation. "First, focus on your posture and breathing. Standing up straight and taking deep breaths will help you project your voice with confidence. Second, slow down your speech and enunciate clearly. This will help you sound more authoritative and in control. Finally, practice regularly so that you can project vocal executive presence naturally and confidently in any situation" (Sicola 2014).

Laura asks in one of her TED talks, "Want to sound like a leader? Start by saying your name right." In the context of how you prepare for next pitch presentation, she continues, "Do you spend 38 percent of your time working on the delivery? If you're like most people, you probably spend the vast majority, if not all, of your time working on the content: your outline, your script, your Power-Point slides, making sure you got cool graphics and some snazzy animations, crunching your data to put into your spreadsheets" (Sicola 2014).

This is especially true for start-up founders working on their pitch decks to present in front of the investors. The focus is on creating the content, and rightly so! After all that work on perfect pitch decks with market information, go to market strategy, and profit models, they sort of wing the delivery hoping it will be good enough. And in the end, that's just comparatively weak, and it can undermine both their immediate goals and objectives as well as their long-term image and reputation.

It is imperative that founders with excellent communication skills are the ones who have the capability to articulate their vision. It's often the little details in communicating your ideas—when you meet with investors or potential partners, for example—that make the biggest impact. Incorporating such communication tools will help build trust among stakeholders, getting them onboard with your start-up initiative or new project before even discussing tangible aspects such as business models or scalability.

Executive presence is another's perception of your success and how a successful leader looks, speaks, and acts. It's the conduit to opportunities.

EVERYONE LOSES WHEN BRILLIANT MINDS UNDERMINE THEMSELVES

"I have been at every table there is, and everyone has doubts. Everyone is scared they are an imposter. The vast majority of these people are amazing—especially the women I meet. I have worked at non-profits, I have been at foundations, I have worked in corporations, served on corporate boards, I have been at G-summits, I have sat in at the UN—they are not that smart." Michelle Obama's speech on the impostor syndrome ignited audiences of all ages. She discussed her own experiences while working in a largely male-dominated sphere, one that saw her underestimated and even doubted at times. This provided Michelle with an intimate knowledge of how powerful figures often feel like frauds despite their storied accomplishments (Young 2022).

Michelle Obama's recent article gave an important reminder that even the most successful of us may feel a sense of imposter syndrome at some point throughout our journey. This is certainly true for start-up founders, who are tasked with creating something from nothing and must believe in themselves to keep going against all odds. Reading Michelle's piece inspired me to start exploring this topic from founders' perspective who may be hurting their potential in building world-changing businesses.

We can all relate to feeling like an imposter. We all have an inner critic who tells us we're not good enough. This is something we share as human beings, but it doesn't always have to stop us from succeeding. By understanding how the inner critic works, and taking action to address it, we can learn how to keep our self-doubt in check and still reach our potential. Making systemic changes to promote greater equity is still important—we need to work together as a society too—but it's also helpful to have ways of outwitting the inner critic on our own terms so that every single one of us can achieve success.

Deepa Purushothaman, author of *The First, the Few, and the Only*, points out that women and people of color have a unique and complicated relationship with power that needs to be examined. In her book, she advocates for "shedding and clearing," which is getting rid of the messages that don't help us and instead creating space for messages that do motivate us to take action. A lot of these messages that aren't beneficial come in the form of telling us to remain patient, be polite, or work harder. For would-be founders from diverse communities, this often conflicts with their goal of raising money or painting the vision of impact they are about to create with their venture.

GET TO NETWORKS THAT EXIST TO BREAK THOSE BOUNDARIES

Swapna's face lit up as she talked about the changes that had allowed diverse communities to make their mark in the business world. She mentioned how Sheeba Demello, who ran the "Women in Investing" group, had created a fantastic opportunity for women to network and gain access to resources that hadn't been available a decade ago. "If you want," Swapna said with a smile, "you can have more of these kinds of networking opportunities. Today, it is an integral component of entrepreneurship ecosystem."

As she spoke, her voice took on a nostalgic tone as she recalled starting out her career. "When I was growing up—and this is India that time—if I had to think of trailblazers, honestly, there were not many. Either there were these large corporates where women were part of family generations, or there was an Indra Nooyi." She paused before continuing, her voice full of hope and excitement. "But now, the situation is different. There are plenty of inspiring women out there, and they are more than willing to help each other out. I've been part of mentorship programs where these women learn from one another. So the world has changed."

She paused for a moment and cleared her throat before continuing, her voice full of conviction. "I think, on the contrary, women can get trapped in a cycle of feeling obligated to satisfy family obligations, when they would rather be networking or expanding their professional horizons." She added, "I do think women are constrained by their own sort of consent, which is to spend time with family versus 'I would rather network,' 'I will do network when it's necessary, or only when it has an outcome,' or 'I will go network just because I have to network.'"

She further added with purpose and force. "Women need to be more aggressive and decisive when it comes to building relationships and not wait for the perfect opportunity. Create it!"

TO BUILD A VENTURE, YOU FIRST NEED TO BE UNAPOLOGETICALLY AMBITIOUS

Shellye Archambeau, former CEO, Fortune 500 board member, and author, believes a lot of success comes from simply letting people know what you want. "I'm a big believer that if you don't tell the universe what you want and what you need, the universe cannot help you" (Archambeau 2020).

As one of the few female African American CEOs in Silicon Valley, Shellye Archambeau knows what it means to own her career. I like how she talks about focusing on defining the goal in a steadfast manner as the first step. To make meaningful progress, don't downplay your achievements or apologize for what you want. Believe in yourself and take ownership of your goals. "You would never spend $3,000 for an airline ticket, pack your bags, board the plane, and then look at the pilot and say, 'So where are we going, anyway?'"

Next step is dedicating yourself to learning the skills necessary to get opportunities that will be important to move your venture forward. Life is full of tough choices, so be intentional about how you spend your money, health, and time in order to achieve what you're aiming for. "It's so easy to become distracted with what is important to someone else," says Shellye. But with a North Star, she's able to cut through the noise, focus in the midst of ambiguity, and spend time on what's most important to her."

"Nobody is born with courage," says Shellye. "Anybody you see who demonstrates courage has developed it, so you can too. When you exhibit courage, you push through." Courage is an essential skill to affect something and rouse others, like getting others to believe in your venture. It's also a muscle that requires frequent testing. Otherwise, we risk succumbing to fear when it matters the most. It's important to keep pushing ourselves out of our comfort zone. These can range from anything like engaging with new people to taking risks with unfamiliar ventures. "I decided I'm going to be the first to raise my hand to step forward and volunteer—because being first to do those things sounds so simple, but honestly, it does take courage."

SILENCE YOUR INNER CRITIC AND SEEK HELP TO FILL GAPS

Without any preparation or education in business, tech, or finance prior to taking the plunge and launching her first tech start-up, Mandela Dixon was at a disadvantage from the very beginning. Financially, she had taken on school and consumer debts and lacked support from wealthy family or friends who could help her get off the ground. She also faced further challenges as a Black female entering what is typically an exclusive environment that lacks diversity at every level of decision making. In 2012, she moved to Silicon Valley and was working on a concept similar to "LinkedIn for Educators."

Later she spent two years as the global director of start-up Weekend Education (2013 through 2015) and became a portfolio services director at venture capital firm Kapor Capital. In 2017, Mandela started Founder Gym, an online training program that teaches underrepresented tech founders how to raise money and grow their start-ups. But despite her success, Mandela says she knew she was different, and early on, that took a toll. "That awareness fueled my impostor syndrome, and for years I hid my differences from other people," Mandela tells CNBC Make It (Clifford 2020).

"When you're an only or one of a few, there is an added pressure to deliver and to not show weakness. You don't want to prove other people's stereotypes right, so you act like everything's okay and you have it all together, even though you could honestly be struggling and could really benefit from getting help." By contrast, "when you are in positions of privilege and power, being vulnerable doesn't usually come with the same baggage or negative connotations that it does for other founders" (Clifford 2020).

Mandela had remained silent about her past. She managed to blend in with her peers who, unlike her, had access to resources and support during their venture into entrepreneurship. This resulted in a realization—in hiding her truth, she was unable to get the help required to make it big. For Mandela Dixon, the biggest learning was that not only did vulnerability open gates of opportunity, but it was essential for success as well. Her experience serves as an important lesson for everyone looking for accomplishment and influence. "Lack of vulnerability is the very thing that prevents you from winning. I learned over the years that the best, most successful founders do one thing better than those who don't succeed: They identify their gaps, and they seek help to fill them," she says (Clifford 2020).

GETTING THROUGH TOUGH CRISIS OF CONFIDENCE

Swapna Gupta talks fondly about her mentors. "My mentors were fabulous. One of my mentors is the reason for whatever I'm doing today. I went to a Kauffman Fellow, and he encouraged me a lot. And that's what I try to do with my peers and subordinates to encourage them." She continues to talk about how we are in a place in a world where, in the newer generation, women are not so left out due to bias. "I think they all have level playing ground in some sense. The world has really evolved to that extent. So it has become more like pay forward to the juniors versus pay forward to a certain section of society like men or women."

I would suspect that entrepreneurs often feel the pressure of expectations from their peers, role models, and the general public, and this pressure can manifest itself as imposter syndrome. This feeling that our accomplishments do not match up to those of influential people like

Steve Jobs, Elon Musk, or Jeff Bezos is a very common experience among entrepreneurs. This feeling of inadequacy may be enhanced by being surrounded by incredibly successful people who have made amazing strides in their respective fields. It becomes harder to adjust one's perception of their quality when they are constantly challenged by individuals far above the average.

I've come to call them self-limiting actions and self-limiting beliefs. Some founders think they need to stay humble and stay out of the spotlight. Minority founders, in particular, often struggle with talking about themselves, believing that it's unbecoming or too boastful. However, neglecting to network and put yourself out there is a self-limiting action that could be impeding your success and preventing you from taking advantage of the right opportunities. I understand the urge to shy away from these tasks, but it's also important to fight against these behaviors if you ever want to break through the glass ceiling.

It's a treacherous cycle we find ourselves in today: Our imposter syndrome stems from an internalization of the biases and patriarchal beliefs we are inundated with. As a coach, I've had to deal with this repeatedly in my clients— an inner critic speaking their truth but reflecting external narratives they have picked up on throughout their lives. Whether it be subtle microaggressions or overt statements of superiority, our self-esteem takes the hit and is left searching for validation. In order to break this cycle and begin authentically believing in ourselves, we must start by acknowledging the real sources of these feeling in order to challenge them at the root cause.

Irrespective of the fact, if you are a founder of color, woman founder, or someone from the majority, it is essential to control the voice in your head that says you are not capable or qualified enough. This inner critic can be damaging to your potential to succeed because it can discourage you from taking risks and initiative, actions which are vital for progressing into positions of authority needed as your start-up scales.

It's crucial to understand this tendency and to do something to fix it. Knowing that many of our insecurities come from this can really help reduce its effect. Also, accept compliments—if people are constantly giving you positive feedback, they really mean it.

The only way to stop feeling like an impostor is to stop thinking like an impostor!

SECTION 4

THE CATALYSTS

CHAPTER 10

ALLYSHIP IS LEADERSHIP: THE (SLOW) RISE OF DIVERSITY IN ENTREPRENEURSHIP

"We have to keep celebrating. We make history not alone but shoulder to shoulder, in allyships that appreciate our obligation to keep the fires lit."

—KC COPELAND

STAKEHOLDERS OF CATALYZING CHANGE

Seated at five feet, seven inches tall, this trim but powerful Black woman tells tales of growing up in modest middle-class family, raised by a single mother. She speaks of the strength she drew from their struggles and the lessons she learned about perseverance, resilience, and self-love. This remarkable woman's confidence was evident in her steady gaze and unwavering voice. As I sit on my side of the laptop screen, it almost feels like being in the same room as her. "I grew up in a lower middle class, but polite, family. We never talked about money. But I was very curious about how people build generational wealth. I had some understanding that the stock market may have something to do with it, but I didn't know what that meant." Vonetta Young is a trailblazer in her profession, proving every day that big things can come in small packages, and where you come from does not define where you go.

Vonetta is an investment readiness and fund formation advisor who helps emerging private equity and venture capital fund managers raise capital confidently and successfully. She advises people of color and women forming their first institutional grade fund, and she calls herself the outsourced chief strategy officer who supports her clients with strategic thinking and storytelling so they can fundraise with ease.

On the wall behind Vonetta, there is a colorful painting of three couples dancing, an image that reflects the joy in her voice. Several books were stacked on a desk behind her, next to the painting. I remember her face so clearly during our conversation, the intensity in her eyes growing with every thought she wanted to express. "I've been a writer since I was a child," she said. "So I wanted to follow my passion for writing. But as I learned more about finance, it just developed into an intellectual curiosity for me. I grew curious about not just how generational wealth is built, but also how income inequality comes about. After my MBA, my ultimate goal was to actually work for a university endowment, so I could 'do well while doing good,' but that just didn't wind up panning out."

She added that she instead got more entrenched in the private equity and venture capital space. "Since the beginning, it was very clear to me there are not a lot of people who look like me in the industry—not a lot of women, and especially not a lot of Black investors. The people who do look like me in the industry are generally the operations managers, or something like that."

And so she worked her way into the investment side as an institutional investor. But she didn't have a great experience in her first stint as investor, largely because she felt so alone as one of few women and people of color at her firm. She had a Latina coworker, but both felt isolated and didn't see opportunities to advance. After a while, she said, neither of them could take the microaggressions any longer, so they both wound up leaving the job.

She seemed slightly sad on my laptop screen as she recalled the memories. "I missed being a little bit of a trailblazer. My coworker and I had this joke that we were trailblazers, which kind of made us feel more comfortable with being the only ones in the room, but also made that the discomfort more obvious to both of us. So that's how I wound up becoming so passionate about what I do. My goal is to get more Black women and people of color to become investors." What started out as just something interesting to learn turned into a passion and mission for Vonetta.

An adage in the industry is that people invest in people who look like themselves. Since there aren't enough women, people of color, or LGBTQ investors, how would entrepreneurs and investors from these minorities ever find support? To change this, Vonetta thought, *How can I arm people who are investors who do happen to look like me? How can I enable them to do the best they can?*

Passion and fervor returned to her voice as she talked about what she does now. "I work with them prior to them raising capital just to make sure they have all their ducks in a row. My ultimate goal was, when these minorities go to an institution for capital, and if the answer is no, it should be only because that institution either doesn't have any money to allocate or because they're racist or sexist, and you can't do anything about any of those things.

"But the folks who have made it into the room and are determined to excel as investors, I asked myself, How can I ensure that they are able to do it authentically and when they hear no, that it's not because of anything that was within their control?" Vonetta's vision is to prepare her fellow community members to be free of any self-limiting actions or beliefs that come in the way of them becoming investors.

TRADITIONAL POWER VERSUS ALLIED POWER

Ever since the inception of humanity, the power struggle has been prevalent. This battle between "traditional power" and "allied power" is a system that is largely unavoidable. Traditional power constantly works to maintain stability, while allied power relentlessly pushes progress forward. The thing that truly sets them apart is where they draw their resources from and how they spend it to get things done.

Allied power surges via collaboration, while traditional power exclusively validates the leader's status and authority. If traditional power has the goal of hoarding its wealth and status, allied power wants to mobilize its force and empower its users.

The realization that the collective influence of many can achieve far greater advances than the actions of a few has enabled countless individuals and organizations to combine efforts; to create a powerful momentum that pushes the boundaries of culture, business, and opportunity. People who work together to channel this power for positive change have the potential be incredibly impactful and successful in pursuit of their goals. Such is the case with allyship that works in tandem with entrepreneurship to drive effective change.

In today's society, it often seems change is impossible. Whether it's working to enact political change or trying to create a more inclusive community, it can feel like the odds are insurmountable. However, history has shown that when people come together and fight for a shared cause, genuine change can occur. All it takes is a collective voice to raise awareness and bring about much-needed reform.

For example, the civil rights movement in the United States was able to effect significant change by uniting people from all walks of life under a banner of equality. Similarly, the #MeToo movement has sparked a worldwide conversation about sexual harassment and assault, leading to new policies and laws that protect victims and hold perpetrators accountable.

These are just two examples of how a community can come together and use its voice to effect positive change. When people work together toward a common goal, they have the power to create lasting social change. In many cases, it only takes a small group of people to get the ball rolling. Once the community has been mobilized, it can effect change on a much larger scale.

BUILD A MOVEMENT

Reshma Saujani views Girls Who Code as a movement. It is a grassroots effort, and she brought that mentality from her advocacy and public service background. The idea for Girls Who Code came about when she was running for office in 2010 in New York City.

In an interview to *Fast Company*, she mentions, "I've always been a policy junky, but when you're actually on the campaign trail, you get to see issues in a much more immediate way. I was visiting schools and talking to teachers and parents across the district, and I saw that our kids weren't learning computer science, and that the gender and socioeconomic divide in tech access was just enormous. With 1.4 million jobs in the computing fields by 2020, I knew we had to do something to close that gap. Women make 85 percent of consumer purchases. When you have women on your team, you will build better, more innovative products that people actually want to buy. It's a no-brainer for businesses" (Saujani 2014). She wanted to inspire girls to be fearless, bold, and, most of all, supportive of one another in building the sisterhood. Her brand voice was built to cultivate a sense of community and participation.

Girls Who Code focuses also on soft skills. The girls learn to pitch their products, present themselves profession-ally, and interact with everyone from a junior engineer to a CEO. As reported in *Wall Street Journal*, in one of her interviews Reshma talks about her background as the daughter of Indian parents who had fled Idi Amin's dictatorship in Uganda to suburban Illinois in the 1970s (Ross 2014). There, she was constantly reminded she was different by the color of her skin and her parents' thick accents. A certain incident of racial and cultural discrim-ination at school led her to having strong feelings about showing up for herself and changing the way she looked and perceived her cultural identity.

When she started high school, she formed a diversity club to educate her fellow students about other cultures. It was the first step on a path that led to an Ivy League education, where she studied law and politics. Ultimately, she started Girls Who Code in 2012. Given her prior experience as a political candidate, Reshma benefitted from the social network and organizational skills necessary to get a nonprofit off the ground. She quickly wrote a business plan and put together a team to start forming a curriculum. In addition, she started meeting with educators and principals to gain their support. However, the most important part of her early planning was securing funding. Within a few years, her organization was up and running and making a difference in the lives of young girls across the country.

THE FIRST, THE FEW, AND THE ONLY HAVE THE POWER TO EMPOWER THE REST

Let me point to some research here: Belonging to the same racial group increases the propensity to work together by 39.2 percent, and having a degree from the same school increases it by 34.4 percent (Gompers and Kovvali 2018). Richard Kerby, one of the few Black venture capitalists in Silicon Valley, analyzed the racial breakdown in VC and found that out of around 1,500 VCs polled, 40 percent had attended either Harvard or Stanford universities (Kerby 2018).

Another research points out that one in five UK VCs went to Oxford, Harvard, or Stanford (Finerva 2019). The homogeneity of the venture capital industry is staggering. A comprehensive data set of every VC organization and investor in the United States since 1990 shows the industry has remained relatively uniform for the past twenty-eight years. Only 8 percent of the investors are women. Racial minorities are also underrepresented—about 2 percent of VC investors are Hispanic, and fewer than 1 percent are Black. This is why it is so hard for women and people of color to break into the industry or get funding from largely white male dominated VC industry.

As per a *Harvard Business Review* article, "The other diversity dividend," nearly three-quarters of VC firms have never hired a woman in that role. What separates that overwhelming majority from the firms that have hired women? One powerful factor is the gender of the partners' children. When a firm's partners have a higher proportion of daughters, the likelihood that a female investor will be hired goes up significantly. Simply replacing one son with a daughter would increase the probability of hiring a woman by 25 percent (Gompers and Kovvali 2018).

Deepa Purushothaman grew up in a very small farm country town, where there wasn't a lot of diversity that she could see. She literally grew up across the cornfield in a countryside in the US, where she belonged to one of the only four families of color in the region. For her there was always a lot of confusion around identity. She went to a school where amongst five hundred kids, there were just four of them who were different. And there was never any talk about race at home.

She said, "As a result of that, I didn't see the same barriers. I always wanted to show I could be in any space and it didn't really matter. I also played soccer on the boys' team until I was in high school, and I was the only girl. I could enter those spaces and compete." For Deepa, it was a combination of those three things of not feeling like she fit in, not really understanding why, and internalizing that. Wanting to focus on this work of raising others like herself made her start this initiative of nFormation Community and writing the book *The First, the Few and the Only.*

NFormation came out of this idea that there is something special in convening women in this way and having conversations about raising each other up. Within the first couple of months, there was waitlist of over one thousand persons to join and be part of the community. Deepa is building a sort of allyship for women of color resounding and resonating with the voices that are coming from these communities. One of the biggest challenges are the flaws on what these communities have been taught about succeeding as individuals; that if you just focus on building your own influence and power and take your company to next level, it's going to be okay.

One of the five principles Deepa is trying to teach is that this is not a lone sport. You're going to need other people, and so cultivating those community relationships as you go is very important. In her book, she calls it "the power of we" (Purushothaman 2022). As she points out, to bring about sustained changes to the power dynamics in the ecosystem, we need to double down on the idea of community networks, yet we've not been taught how or where to do that. From her experience when she talks with women, most of them would talk about the fact they came from societies where there was a real focus on community and not just individual success.

She highlights an important point: "Having these kinds of conversations about things you've been taught and the things that are important to you don't have to be separate from how you do this." More importantly, she ensured to multiply the message through her initiative in raising other women up who might have felt what she herself felt once. She is currently also leading a virtual initiative, "Raising our voice: Your next steps," where she is sharing action-oriented advice on how women of color could make the most of opportunities available to them.

FORMS OF ALLYSHIP—MENTORSHIP AND SPONSORSHIP

Mentorship is another important part of allyship. By sharing your knowledge and experiences with someone who is just starting out, you can help them avoid some of the mistakes you made and give them the tools they need to succeed. Allyship is not a one-time act. It's a lifelong commitment to making the world a more equitable place for everyone. Allies that come from the already privileged backgrounds can also play a crucial role in mentoring and supporting diverse entrepreneurs, countering sexism and other forms of discrimination, and using their power to support businesses that empower others.

Shivangi Walke wanted to benefit women's communities. She started Thrive with Mentoring, where she brings around four hundred women to the platform every year in one-on-one mentoring relationships. It is a nonprofit organization, where most volunteers are from corporates in high leadership positions. She has been running this organization, which is completely bootstrapped for almost five years now, with close to two hundred volunteers. It's a bit unbelievable for people because most do nonprofits only if they are funded by somebody. But Shivangi used her powerful voice, brand, and capability to bring networks together to shape a vibrant global community of successful women who support, encourage, and empower each other to succeed professionally and personally.

In my interview with her, she mentions candidly, "Most people I interact with on my commercial part of the business are men, and I really believe I have maybe been blind to that because I have personally quite a few masculine qualities that are also somehow linked to my upbringing. I grew up with a very strong mother. She was a banker, and I grew up in India."

Shivangi talked about how she was already in the top forty people in a forty thousand people company in her early thirties—and the only woman on the executive level. "I actually went up the corporate ladder pretty steep, pretty quick. I have also not suffered in my life much from imposter syndrome. It's a phenomenon that I became aware of because of Thrive. We know that confidence is valued more than competence. I'm not saying I was not competent, but I was also extremely confident."

She also reflects on how she never faced any biases or felt like she came from an underrepresented group. "I must say that when I was working in corporate, which I did for seventeen years, I was blissfully unaware of biases. I became hyper aware of these biases after I left corporate and after I started my own business, and even more after I started with Thrive with Mentoring initiative. That's when I said to myself that I want to do something for women. A woman helped me tremendously when I went through a really tough phase. I just thought there is some magic in women to women mentoring."

She recognizes the privileges and opportunities available to her and is grateful for them, yet she is aware that life can be much more difficult for others who face inequalities and bigoted stereotypes. She chooses to use her position of power to uplift others and leave a legacy of inclusion.

SUBTLE, INTENTIONAL CHANGES CAN HAVE RIPPLE EFFECTS THAT ARE FELT THROUGHOUT

A study by Gueorgi Kossinets and Duncan J. Watts, on "Origins of Homophily in an Evolving Social Network," found that e-mail communication patterns can be a proxy for social connections and that these connections have a large impact on the levels of diversity within groups

(Kossinets and Watts 2009). The study found that activities such as taking new classes, joining new activities, or even minor individual tendencies to interact with similar people could have a large cumulative effect, resulting in striking levels of group homogeneity.

This research suggests it is important to encode diversity into organizational structures from the outset in order to avoid further entrenching existing disparities. On the other hand, anyone who has ever been in a group knows the dynamic can change quickly when new people are added to the mix. The same is true of small groups of people who wield outsize decision-making authority.

Whether it's venture capital or group of successful founders, bringing just a few talented women or racial minorities into the group can change the relative balance of power. And when the balance of power shifts, so does the way decisions are made. Suddenly, issues that were previously overlooked come to the fore, and dissenting voices are given more weight. The result is that even subtle, intentional changes can have ripple effects that are felt throughout. Even though it may seem like a small shift, adding just a few diverse voices can have a big impact.

Olatowun Candide-Johnson is someone I met recently who is creating such ripple effects across her community. Olatowun inspired me with her GAIA AFRICA initiative that she has created in the form of a private club. GAIA AFRICA is Nigeria's premier private members business club for women decision makers, established to serve Africa's top 5 percent of female C-suite executives, business founders, senior professionals, creatives, and public officers.

Ola's Vision is "to contribute to the socio-economic growth and transformation of Africa by empowering women to organize around the principles of female leadership and participation in business." Ola puts it in perspective for me that, as per a McKinsey & Company report, "societies that continue to allow gender gap leave tons of cash on the table and that just by narrowing that gap could add $12 trillion to the 2025 global GDP. However, women must meet this challenge head on by leveraging their own strengths in collaboration with their peers." She is on a mission to bridge that gap through this private membership club she offers, where women in decision-making positions connect, share interests, collaborate, partner, learn together, support, and sponsor one another while they're lifelong friendships and collaborations.

When I asked Ola about her journey and how she created such a powerful venture, she mentioned about the case studies she was inspired by while doing her MBA. "I'm reading about these people—human beings who have one head, and two eyes, one nose and a mouth. And I'm reading about these people who are doing these amazing things. I must be able to do something as well. I am no different! Honestly, that really also taught me—you shouldn't really do anything on a small scale. It's got to be bigger than you, right? The dream has got to be bigger, the vision has to be bigger than me, in order to do it!"

She further talked about the initiative and what motivated her to start. "I wondered—why is it that women can connect on so many different levels, but they don't really connect when it comes to business? They don't really pass business to one another and were not really collaborating in business. And that's what I wanted to change! I knew that there had to be a clubhouse so that they have their own space to meet, mingle, and connect regularly.

"I knew that we had to have the mini clubs (smaller interest groups), because when these members meet, it's great to connect over something familiar. Something they both have an interest in. Without relationship, they're never going to build trust. And if they don't build trust, they're never going to fulfil the vision, which is to form alliances, do business together, or sponsor each other for business deals, board seats, and the like. I have to inculcate this mindset. And this initiative is important to move the needle to closing the gender economic gap. I know that when women are doing a lot more than they're doing today, it will always trickle down."

HOMOPHILIC BIAS DISPLAYED BY MINORITIES CREATES MORE INCLUSIVE NETWORKS

Many people may assume that when members of underrepresented groups show favoritism toward those most similar to themselves (as in the case of most examples in this chapter), they are doing so in a way that negates any progress made toward greater diversity. Although, the truth is quite the opposite. When homophilic bias is displayed by these groups, it can actually be used to create even larger, more inclusive networks. This is done by allowing members of those same underrepresented groups to openly support and work with each other, thus providing access to resources and opportunities not previously available. Ultimately, when such biases become beneficial instead of problematic, every individual can benefit from a more diverse ecosystem.

If you belong to the overrepresented group, you can start by committing to learn more about the marginalized communities you want to support. Listen to their stories and experiences. Research the issues they're facing. For those who have been trailblazers in their underrepresented communities, engaging in peer learning is a powerful tool, as we have seen in the examples of Reshma, Deepa, Ola, and Shivangi in this chapter.

When minority founders are successful, they create positive examples that others can emulate and build upon. These trailblazing founders (role models) also demonstrate the viability of non-traditional paths to success, potentially inspiring more people from these backgrounds to pursue entrepreneurship. Founders could also start smaller initiatives to meet maybe once a quarter to share leads or things that have been helpful to advance their goals. And this alone can create community.

One can simply start by sharing inspirational stories of minority founders with the world, something that Shradha Sharma of YourStory demonstrated beautifully. Role models are vital within the entrepreneurial world.

They serve as powerful reminders of what has already been accomplished and what has yet to be done. This is exactly what I hope to achieve through the medium of this book and bringing forward stories of diverse role models to inspire. There is something special about hearing a first-hand account of someone's journey to success and what steps they took to get there. Perhaps it is the sense of connection that we feel, or the reminder that anything is possible if we are willing to do what it takes to succeed.

For individuals from disadvantaged or underprivileged backgrounds, these stories from Tope, Shradha, Babu, and Maria can be especially motivating. They demonstrate that it is possible to overcome adversity and achieve great things, no matter where you come from. By sharing these stories, we can help to empower and inspire others to pursue their entrepreneurial dreams. Additionally, we can shine a spotlight on the unique contributions these founders have made to the economy and to the society.

We sometimes don't think about doing those things because we're so busy and so focused on not sharing what we know. But focusing on what we know can often change things for the whole community. It may feel slower in the beginning, but a community and this idea of allyship, at some point, can accelerate your own success as well.

Tristan Walker ended his conversation with Kevin Cool in his interview by saying, "I have a burden of responsibility for an audience I care so deeply about, because I recognize the power of my representation. And it's important that if I maintain the values I have, I'm doing my best. I can't fulfill expectations that people have of me that I can't have for myself. And the only expectation I have for myself is making decisions I can be proud of" (Cool 2022).

He knows better than anyone how powerful representation can be and how much it matters to those who look up to him. His words resonated deeply with those listening and were a powerful reminder that we can all strive to take on roles of influence in our communities and places where we hope to make an impact. His serves as an inspiring story that encourages hope and optimism to all who aspire toward working on a greater representation in the entrepreneurship ecosystem.

"I think the future is founders who care about the tribes they want to build and sticking with it, because that's a big enough opportunity" —Tristan Walker (James 2023).

CONCLUSION

TO HEAR BOLD STORIES, WE NEED BRAVE STORYTELLERS

"First and foremost, you need to get out of your own way."

—JEFFREY PFEFFER

To hear new stories, we need new storytellers. Entrepreneurship is as old as time (the wheel was invented too!), but society reached a stagnation point because the same stories were being uplifted and told repeatedly. That is now changing, and this book is one tile on the path toward that change. It contributes to a larger movement toward true innovation and growth. It is a gateway to new conversations and possibilities and a symbol of the never-ending cycle of the invention that defines our species.

The purpose of this book was clear—to shine a spotlight on the often challenging but deeply rewarding journey of entrepreneurs. I wanted to honor the heroic trailblazer founders who have taken on the challenge of changing the status quo, no matter the odds. These stories prove that anything is possible when ambition and courage come together. We must remember the impact we make and the difference we leave behind—these are the things that will truly help us be remembered.

At the end of 2021, Align Capital Partners (ACP) acquired a portion of We Are Rosie in a deal valuing the company at $110 million. While the past few years have felt like setback after setback, stories like We Are Rosie's might signal a more optimistic future. After all, in 2021, Sara Blakely became a billionaire, along with Falguni Nayar, who became the wealthiest self-made female billionaire in India. Reese Witherspoon's Hello Sunshine sold for $900 million, demonstrating value in celebrating minority stories (Shoenthal 2022).

Inspired by these stories, I started this mission to motivate founders with evidence-based approaches to achievement, convincing them to rely on themselves and to understand the essential value of what they are building. I took it upon myself to highlight the stories of Riddhiman Das, Shradha Sharma, Tristan Walker, Babu Sivadasan, Lisa Shu, Tope Awotona, Deepa Purushothaman, Reshma Saujani, Radhika Iyengar, Claudia Mitchell, and many others in this book that stand as a beacon of hope. Each achieved extraordinary success, forging an unbreakable path celebrating their uniqueness and difference.

As entrepreneurs, we are not as alone or lost as we might feel. Where others might tell themselves a story with implicit assumptions and inherited limitations, a true leader sees an opportunity with calculated risk to innovate and improve the world.

Riddhiman Das's story of transformation and resilience stirred something inside. With a potent brand, a never-ending will to break stereotypes, and a strong presence in the room, Das emerged as a powerful entrepreneur. The intense struggle of Shradha Sharma's journey and the ultimate success spoke of pure perseverance that indelibly lit a fire in those who heard it. She held onto hope, defying the odds and eventually achieving her goal, a triumphant victory of spirit and will.

Tristan Walker succeeded not in spite of stereotypes but regardless of them. He cultivated familiarity, capability, and confidence to navigate the founder's ecosystem. Even though most start-ups are doomed to the scrap heap of history, investors have been willing to fund his vision, in no small part, because most people prefer to make money while also doing good. Calendly founder Tope Awotona's story highlights some crucial learnings from his toolkit. While networking is essential, he highlighted founders could engage networks through traction and brand building. He effectively built traction and business before getting investors to prove his idea's worth.

Shellye Archambeau distilled the essence of entrepreneurship with this clarion call to action: define the goal; dedicate yourself to learning skills and cultivate opportunities; and remember that "nobody is born with courage." You have to develop it.

We must learn to step out of our comfort zones. In order to accomplish anything of value, we must become comfortable with being uncomfortable. We were in awe of SC Moatti's inspiring story—an immigrant and woman who smashed the Silicon Valley glass ceiling to become a successful investor. She enlightened us on the "join, shape, drive" framework of building a personal brand, stressing how it can bridge the gap between everyday people and elite power circles.

The funding is out there—right now. If anything, investors are motivated less by skin color and gender identity and more by FOMO (fear of missing out) to back a winning enterprise. Taking action can be the catalyst to unearth the hidden potential within yourself and in the world around you. Start here:

1. **First and foremost, get out of your own way to find your way in.** Investors are interested in people behind ideas who can make them a reality. They seek out entrepreneurs with the potential to bring their investments ten times the return. This book illuminates social science research and behavioral patterns to help you ascend above the competition and conquer common biases. Do not get comfortable in the *stereotypes* you are in. Take control of your future!

2. **Build courage.** If you are ambitious, you need to raise your risk tolerance. However, this is not just any kind of risk-taking but the kind that requires courage. Courage is not something you are born with. It develops by getting out of your way. And you do this by

constantly putting yourself in uncomfortable situations. It is a muscle that you need to exercise regularly. The more you do it, the easier it becomes.

3. **Persist a little longer.** The need for achievement is often motivated by a desire for personal satisfaction and a sense of accomplishment rather than any external rewards. This urge can push you to take chances and seize possibilities, no matter how daunting the odds may be. Link your ambition to your goal to keep your fire burning.

4. **People matter and are the only currency of success.** Entrepreneurs should relentlessly and strategically develop relationships with as many people as possible. We must never forget that our success is directly linked to the networks we build and cultivate. Nothing in life is truly achieved without the influence of those around us.

5. **Polish your executive presence.** It matters, and it is challenging to develop! There are biases we all cannot fight, but if we know what works—we have extra tools to help us look powerful. You can choose what you do with the information you have. You can use the combination of cognitive, emotional, and physical presence to stand out as confident and self-assured and develop the ability to inspire confidence among your teams, clients, partners, and investors.

6. **Defeat imposter syndrome:** It is a natural phenomenon affecting people of all cultures and genders. The

inner critic often amplifies these messages, leading us to believe we are not good enough or do not belong. We must also learn to silence the inner critic and practice self-compassion. Only then can we begin to achieve our full potential. We all have a mental picture of ourselves, and that picture can influence our behavior and how we interact with others. It is essential to inventory the words we use to describe ourselves. Are they accurate or outdated? Are they uplifting or disempowering? It is essential to rewire our self-image with words of affirmation and power, leading to a transformed outlook on life and unlocking our full potential.

7. **Build a brand called *You*:** With the advent of social media, customers and clients, and even VCs, are more likely to engage with businesses they identify with on a personal level. As a founder, projecting your credibility and that of your start-up from its initial stages is essential. It is important to remember that shyness and non-self-promotion raises walls. If you are not self-promoting, it is not them—it is you! You must kick the door open and join in the conversation. If you do not know what to say, ask questions. You can build the company and brand you want by taking the initiative and engaging with others.

8. **Have allyship.** We cannot do it alone. Like most professional endeavors, growing entrepreneurship is ideally bolstered by a social network. While I wish I could say underrepresented founders intrinsically have everything they need to excel, I believe we

require allies and support beyond basic networking and spanning gender and race. It is not enough to have a more significant number of diverse founders in the start-up world. We also need to see a spike in the diversification of VCs. More representation in VC means more representation for founders. You want to be in power because you have the potential and position to empower those who need that visibility.

As the anthropologist Margaret Mead once said, "Never doubt that a small group of thoughtful, committed citizens can change the world. Indeed, it is the only thing that ever has" (Ryder 2001). The potential of transformation and the power of wise action count. Gaze upon the world, and it might seem unchangeable and inconceivable. It is not. It can be shifted with a little push in just the ideal place.

I hope that I have inspired you through this book to take action and acknowledge that our minds and hearts are capable of powerful transformation. A new way forward means we cannot hold on too tightly to our self-defeating thoughts.

- As individuals, communities, and societies, we must ask ourselves: What stories are we telling ourselves? What stories are we inhabiting and living by?
- We must use this power to shatter the invisible boundaries that keep us from achieving our goals.
- We must bravely promote new ideas, new narratives, and new storytellers.

ACKNOWLEDGMENTS

I am grateful to the many people who believed in these ideas and gave so much of themselves to make the publication of *Trailblazer Founders* possible.

In writing this book, I had the opportunity to interview many start-up founders, all of whom granted me exclusive access to their stories. I felt the intensity of their journey as I spoke with them, humbled by their courage to share them with the world. I was also honored to have several conversations with seasoned VCs, journalists, and industry experts within the start-up innovation, many of whom have permitted me to use their names. Thank you for taking time out of your busy schedules to share what you know with me and the world. Every conversation was an invaluable learning experience that left me itching to learn more. Without their help, this book would never have been possible.

My sincerest gratitude goes to Professor Jeffrey Pfeffer and his work on "Building Power," which profoundly influenced my professional life. His teachings have been instrumental in helping me comprehend how people can become their own barrier. As a coach in his Executive Education program at Stanford University's Graduate School of Business, the insights I have acquired have been invaluable. I am now providing it in this book, specifically tailored to those in the world of start-ups and entrepreneurship. He was the first person to support me on this book project, helping me brainstorm themes and encouraging me to explore further depths when it came to research and studies. Without his teachings, I wouldn't have learned all the principles of power, much less be able to write this book today.

This whole thing of writing a book happened because of Renaud Falgas, who inspired me to bring my ideas to life. I am grateful for his friendship, as well as for his supportive check-in calls throughout my author journey. He has contributed materials and stimulated my thinking about the subject.

This book was made possible because people have provided unwavering support and sincere, constructive feedback throughout my writing journey. I want to thank Helio Mosquim Junior, Greg Singer, Robin Coleman, Philip Mohabir, and Inbal Demri for spending hours reading my chapters and helping me make sense of the content of this book.

I had the privilege of working with Robin Coleman at a health-tech start-up, and his input on all topics we worked on significantly impacted my thinking. He devoted his valuable time and energy to giving me regular feedback and acting as a mentor and a guide. His expertise as an acquisitions editor at Johns Hopkins University Press drew me away from the abstract, allowing me to refine the communication of complex themes with simple principles. He helped me tap into emotion's power to drive my ideas home. I am humbled by his willingness to share his wisdom.

I have had the good fortune of working with Philip Mohabir and Inbal Demri as my peers as executive coaches at Stanford University's Graduate School of Business. They believed in this project so much that they dedicated many hours for months before I fully committed. They were instrumental in helping flesh out the initial ideas and turning those ideas into outlines. They were also insightful and generous with their suggestions about the chapter titles. It is an honor and privilege to work with them.

Helio Mosquim Junior, also my peer as executive coach at Stanford University's Graduate School of Business, who over the years I have also come to know as a friend, has been a great source of encouragement for this book. Not only has he provided insightful feedback during my chapter revisions, but he and his brother, Alexandre Augusto Mosquim, have even gone so far as to become ambassadors of this book in Brazil's innovation ecosystem.

Mikel Mangold played a massive role in beginning my book. He showed me the resources, strategies, and publishing crew I needed to complete the project. He has always been there with encouragement and advice whenever I hit a roadblock or needed a second opinion.

I'd like to recognize Elizabeth MacBride's contribution to this book. She was one of the first people I spoke to while researching the themes I covered in this book, and she helped shape my way of presenting the lives of trailblazer founders. Elizabeth's representation of how women and minorities can be role models significantly impacted how this book was written. I want to thank her for her insight as the founder and editor of *The Times of Entrepreneurship* and her personal experience writing a book.

So many others have been kind and given their time to read drafts, share ideas, or help me take my first steps into writing this book. I'd like to thank Emilie White, Theresa Lina, Juana-Catalina Rodriguez, Lauren Krasny, Austin Ramsland, Michael Wenderoth, Nana Fatima Paturel, Monika-Staszewska-Kruk, Samia Qamar, Michael Presley, Nirali Shah, Shruti Parashar, Poornima Gopi, Petya Rasheva, Aneesh Madani, Akshay Ahuja, Rodrigo Ferreira, Hector Gusmão, Rogerio Toscano, Paulo Rocca, Diane O'Reilly, Martina Nicodemo, Andres F. Marquez, Nick Lamela, Penny Peavler, and Sofia Toteva for their generosity. Fernando Suzuki, in particular, offered thoughts on how he sees this as a fourth wall in theatre, which inspired me to start the introduction of my book with this analogy.

My deepest gratitude to Eric Koester and his entire editorial, design, and marketing team, whose unflagging support kept this project on the fast track.

Manish Bansal, Disha Goel Wilde, and Parul Bahirwani have a special place in my heart. They are my closest friends and the most honest critics. Throughout my writing journey, they have been generous with their time and given me valuable feedback, advice, and support.

The unlimited support of my family has been the foundation of my life. My immense appreciation and affection also go out to my mother, Renu Gulati. When I was on the cusp of a strenuous eight-week book revisions period, she just happened to be visiting—and she performed a wondrous feat. She took charge of the household so I could remain focused and complete the book. For this generous act of love, I will always be grateful. My father, Anil K. Gulati, and my sister, Nidhi Arora, have been a steady source of motivation throughout my life and have always been enthusiastic about my pursuits.

And finally, I want to thank my incredible husband, Monish, from reading early drafts to giving me advice on the cover and fueling me with copious amounts of coffee to keep me writing past the midnight hours. He was as important to this book getting done as I was. I began this book with my son, Kabir Pahwa, inside me. My husband gave his love and patience equally to both my "babies": Kabir and *Trailblazer Founders*. Thank you so much!

Special thanks to all my backers that stepped forward with over two hundred pre-orders for this book before it was even real. They made the time and effort to care, despite the busyness of life. I am forever thankful to all of you for your unique contributions, and I'm committed to keeping my promise of naming all the people involved (in alphabetical order by first name):

Abhijatya Dhamija
Abhishek Bhat
Alain Brunschwiler
Aleksandr Sokoletsky
Alexandre Augusto Mosquim
Alina Adams
Allison Wilkinson
Amy Pragel
Ana-Luiza Georgescu
Andres Marquez
Aneesh Madani
Angela Freitas
Annie Joh
Anupma Mangla
Archana Sharma
Armand Cacacho
Audrey Lazar
Austin Ramsland
Binay K Jha
Chris Smith
D.G Wilde
Daniel Matthies
Deepti Madhok
Elena Pronicheva
Emilie White
Eric Koester
Erik Nilsen
Gayatri Babbar
Graham Swanepoel
Greg Singer
Gwenael Hannema, InnoSpina
Harald Nuhn

Harpreet Bhatia
Helio Mosquim Junior
Irina Nicoleta Scarlat
Irshad Saifi
Javier Ortiz
Jessica Lum
Joao Dassoler
Juan Elices
Juana-Catalina Rodriguez
Juanita Pied
Julia Jaysan
Julien Delvat
Justin Beck
Kanuj Gakhar
Karthik Kumar
Karthik Venkat
Kateryna Mikula
Katharina Mahadeva
Kathrin Chimm
Kaushal Mehta
Kent Mar
Kevin Williams
Lulu Raghavan
Madhavi Rajan
Manish Bansal
Manisha Bhalekar
Marcus Fornell
Maria Castellon
Markus May
Martin Spycher
Martina Nicodemo
Marwan Al Kinj

Maurice Oduor
Maya Ramati Grossi
Michael Presley
Mikel Mangold
Mini Suri
Mirjam Seckler
Misha Bykov
Mohinder Sikka
Moinuddin Mohammed
Nalin Chaturvedi
Nana Fatima Paturel
Nawal Vikram
Nicholas Lamela
Nidhi Arora
Nikhil Sharma
Nils Frohloff
Nirali Shah
Nizar Kheraj
Olatowun Candide-Johnson
Olga Fontanellaz
Parul Katyal
Philip Brouwer
Phillip Mohabir
Piyush Goel
Poornima Gopi
Priya Tamhankar
Priyanshu Gupta
Rainer Hehmann
Raj Shiva
Raja Basu
Randa Elbarbari
Renaud Falgas

Ricardo Perez Font
Robert Herman
Robin Coleman
Rutooj Deshpande
Samet Karadag
Samia Qamar
Samuel Hayes
Sanjay Dabur
Schaffter Célia
Sherif Elbarrad
Shruti Parashar
Shyam Santhanam
Sofiya Toteva
Sriram Natarajan
Stefan Godly
Switzerland Innovation Park Basel Area
Thidar Swe Tin
Thomas Fahy
Tiphaine Charretier
Tushar Kansal
Uros Lekic
Vajeeha Tabassum
Valerie Andrey
Vidya Battu
Vinesh Korlakunta
Vivek Dixit
Wayne Cheung
Xinjin Zhao

APPENDIX

INTRODUCTION

Blee, Bob, Andrew Pardo, Calvin Otis, and Eli Oftedal. 2021. "State of the Markets Report Q1 2021." Santa Clara, CA: Silicon Valley Bank. https://www.svb.com/trends-insights/reports/state-of-the-markets-report/q1-2021.

Makinson, Rachel. 2021. "How Spanx Founder Sara Blakely Created a Billion-Dollar Brand." *CEO Today*, October 28, 2021. https://www.ceotodaymagazine.com/2021/10/how-spanx-founder-sara-blakely-created-a-billion-dollar-brand/.

Ross, Kathryn, and Tom Lounibos. 2022. "Bridging the Black Founders Venture Capital Gap." *Technology* (blog), Accenture. February 16, 2022. https://www.accenture.com/us-en/insights/technology/black-founders.

Singh, Tushar Deep. 2021. "How Falguni Nayar Built NYKAA to Stand out from the Crowd." *The Economic Times*, 12, November 2021. https://economictimes.indiatimes.com/tech/

startups/who-is-falguni-nayar-indias-richest-self-made-woman/articleshow/87629451.cms.

Taylor, Kiara. 2022. "Legendary Black Entrepreneurs." *Business Leaders* (blog), Investopedia. December 31, 2022. https://www.investopedia.com/legendary-black-entrepreneurs-5112876.

Teare, Gené 2020. "Global VC Funding to Female Founders Dropped Dramatically This Year." *Crunchbase News* (blog), 21 Dec. 2020. https://news.crunchbase.com/news/global-vc-funding-to-female-founders/.

CHAPTER 1 THE SMART MONEY—VC INSIDERS' TAKE ON THE "INVESTABLE JOCKEY"

Rowley, Jason. 2017. "Where and Why Venture Capitalists Invest Close to Home." *Venture* (blog), *TechCrunch*. November 16, 2017. https://techcrunch.com/2017/11/16/where-and-why-venture-capitalists-invest-close-to-home/.

CHAPTER 2 THE JOCKEY VS THE HORSE— WHAT COMPELS THE INVESTMENT DECISION

Bernstein, Shai, Arthur G. Korteweg, and Kevin Laws. 2015. "Attracting Early Stage Investors: Evidence from a Randomized Field Experiment." *Journal of Finance* 72, no. 2 (April): 509-538. http://doi.org/10.2139/ssrn.2432044.

Bussgang, Jeffrey. 2011. *Mastering the VC Game: A Venture Capital Insider Reveals How to Get from Start-up to IPO on Your Terms*. Alberta, Canada: Portfolio.

Dewar, Carolyn, Scott Keller, and Vik Malhotra. 2021. "Author Talks: What Separates the Best CEOS from the Rest?" Interviewed by Raju Narisetti. *Insights* (blog), McKinsey and Company. December 15, 2021. https://www.mckinsey.com/featured-insights/mckinsey-on-books/author-talks-what-separates-the-best-ceos-from-the-rest.

Gompers, Paul A., Will Gornall, Steven N. Kaplan, and Ilya A. Strebulaev. 2016. "How Do Venture Capitalists Make Decisions?" *Journal of Financial Economics* 135, no. 1 (January): 169-190. http://doi.org/10.2139/ssrn.2801385.

Strebulaev, Ilya. 2016. "Jockeys Trump Horses in Race to Secure VC Funding." *Entrepreneur* (blog), *VentureBeat*. December 18, 2016. https://venturebeat.com/entrepreneur/jockeys-trump-horses-in-race-to-secure-vc-funding/.

Teeter, Darius. 2022. "The Psychology of Power and Influence." Stanford Seed, *Insights* (blog), Stanford Graduate School of Business. April 12, 2022. https://www.gsb.stanford.edu/insights/psychology-power-influence.

CHAPTER 3 POWER AND INFLUENCE—BUILD IT BEFORE YOU NEED IT

Horowitz, Ben. 2010. "Why We Prefer Founding CEOs." *Executive Talent* (blog), *Andreessen Horowitz*. April 28, 2010. https://a16z.com/2010/04/28/why-we-prefer-founding-ceos/.

James, Yan. 2023. "Tristan Walker, CEO of Walker and Company: The Problem with Sameness." Stanford Graduate School of Business. February 3, 2023. 51:39. https://youtu.be/NNO8tH07EH0.

Weissmann, Jordan. 2013. "Entrepreneurship: The Ultimate White Privilege?" *The Atlantic*, August 2013. https://www.theatlantic.com/business/archive/2013/08/entrepreneurship-the-ultimate-white-privilege/278727/.

CHAPTER 4 MAKING BOLD MOVES— NEUTRALIZING FOUNDER STEREOTYPE THREATS EARLY

Azevedo, Mary Ann. 2019. "Untapped Opportunity: Minority Founders Still Being Overlooked." *Diversity* (blog), *Crunchbase News*. February 27, 2019. https://news.crunchbase.com/news/untapped-opportunity-minority-founders-still-being-overlooked/.

Gupta, Vishal K., Daniel B. Turban, S. Arzu Wasti, and Arijit Sikdar. 2009. "The Role of Gender Stereotypes in Perceptions of Entrepreneurs and Intentions to Become an Entrepreneur." *Entrepreneurship Theory and Practice* 33, no. 2 (March): 397–417. https://doi.org/10.1111/j.1540-6520.2009.00296.x.

Kanze, Dana, Laura Huang, Mark Conley, and Tony Higgins. 2021. "Male and Female Entrepreneurs Get Asked Different Questions by VCS—and It Affects How Much Funding They Get." *Harvard Business Review*, September 2021. https://hbr.org/2017/06/male-and-female-entrepreneurs-get-asked-different-questions-by-vcs-and-it-affects-how-much-funding-they-get.

Katsarou, Maria. 2022. "Women and the Leadership Labyrinth Howard vs Heidi." *Leadership Psychology Institute* (blog). Accessed February 25, 2023. https://www.leadershippsychologyinstitute.com/women-the-leadership-labyrinth-howard-vs-heidi/.

Morgan Stanley. 2019. "Beyond the VC Funding Gap." *Inclusive Innovation and Opportunity* (blog), *Morgan Stanley*. October 23, 2019. https://www.morganstanley.com/ideas/venture-capital-funding-gap/.

Morris, Michael H., Donald F. Kuratko, and Minet Schindehutte. 2016. "Towards Integration: Understanding Entrepreneurship through Frameworks." *The International Journal of Entrepreneurship and Innovation* 2, no. 1 (November): 35–49. https://doi.org/10.5367/000000001101298765.

Williams, Lara. 2021. "Opinion: Venture Capital Firms Are Blind to the Benefits of Diversity." *ESG* (blog), *Investment Monitor*. April 7, 2021. https://www.investmentmonitor.ai/esg/venture-capital-firms-blind-benefits-diversity/

Clarke, Tessa. 2022. "Building a Founder Brand Is Your Job. Here's How to Do It." start-up *Life* (blog), *Sifted*. November 6, 2022. https://sifted.eu/articles/tessa-olio-founder-brand/.

Clear, James (@JamesClear). 2019. "Investors Famously Look for Ideas that are 'huge, if true.'" Twitter, 1:04 AM Apr 19, 2019, https://twitter.com/JamesClear/status/1119013772511850497.

Cool, Kevin. 2022. "Tristan Walker." *MBA Alumni* (blog), Stanford Graduate School of Business. July 15, 2022. https://www.gsb.stanford.edu/programs/mba/life-community/alumni/voices/tristan-walker.

Dewar, Carolyn, Scott Keller, and Vik Malhotra. 2021. "Author Talks: What Separates the Best CEOS from the Rest?" Interviewed by Raju Narisetti. *Insights* (blog), McKinsey and Company. December 15, 2021. https://www.mckinsey.com/featured-insights/mckinsey-on-books/author-talks-what-separates-the-best-ceos-from-the-rest.

Handley, Lucy. 2019. "Ariana Huffington: Media Mogul, Lifelong Learner." *The Brave Ones* (blog), *CNBC*. October 28, 2019. https://www.cnbc.com/arianna-huffington-from-author-and-media-mogul-to-founder-of-thrive/.

Pfeffer, Jeffrey. 2016. "Tristan Walker: The Extroverted Introvert." *Case Studies* (blog), Stanford Graduate School of Busi-

ness. 2016. https://www.gsb.stanford.edu/faculty-research/
case-studies/tristan-walker-extroverted-introvert.

Stollery, Paul. 2022. "Coverage to Capital—Unicorn Edition:
Does a CEO's Presence on Social Media Impact Their Ability to Fundraise?" *Agency News* (blog), *Hard Numbers*.
Accessed February 27, 2022. https://hardnumbers.co.uk/
news/hard-numbers/coverage-to-capital-unicorn-edition-
does-a-ceos-presence-on-social-media-impact-their-ability-
to-fundraise/.

Walker, Tristan. 2014. "Where Entrepreneurs Find Inspiration," Interviewed by Tina Seelig. Released April 9, 2014
for *eCorner* (blog), Stanford University. Video, 56:59. https://
ecorner.stanford.edu/videos/be-an-authentic-entrepre-
neur-entire-talk.

Warnock, Eleanor. 2022. "Want to Raise More Cash for Your
start-up? Post on Linkedin." start-up *Life* (blog), *Sifted*.
November 30, 2022. https://sifted.eu/articles/founder-linke-
din-funding/.

Yan, James. 2023. "Tristan Walker, CEO of Walker and Company: The Problem with Sameness." Stanford Graduate
School of Business. February 3, 2023. 51:39. https://youtu.
be/NNO8tHo7EHo.

Awotona, Tope. 2020. "Tope Awotona, Founder Calendly,
   start-up Runway Keynote | Valor Ventures." Interviewed
   by Valor Ventures. November 18, 2020. 29:40 https://www.
   youtube.com/watch?v=8jgOc9XgQog.

Burt, Ronald S. 1992. *Structural Holes: The Social Structure of
   Competition.* Cambridge, MA: Harvard University Press.

Ferrazzi, Keith, and Tahl Raz. 2014. *Never Eat Alone: And Other
   Secrets to Success, One Relationship at a Time.* New York, NY:
   Currency.

Ibarra, Herminia. 2016. "Building Effective Networks." YouTube.
   Herminia Ibarra. March 24, 2016. 15:06. https://www.you-
   tube.com/watch?v=k115ePA_9SU.

Prince, Sara, and Tawanda Sibanda. 2022. "Being Intentional and
   Being Lucky: An Interview with Barry Lawson Williams."
   People and Organizational Performance (blog), McKinsey
   and Company. January 28, 2022. https://www.mckinsey.
   com/business-functions/people-and-organizational-per-
   formance/our-insights/being-intentional-and-being-lucky-
   an-interview-with-barry-lawson-williams.

CHAPTER 7 PERSIST A LITTLE LONGER— FOCUS, DETERMINATION, AND WILL TO SUCCEED

Feldman, Amy. 2022. "Nigeria-Born Tope Awotona Poured His Life Savings into Calendly. Now He's One of America's Wealthiest Immigrants." *Forbes Magazine*, April/May 2022. https://www.forbes.com/sites/amyfeldman/2022/04/06/nigeria-born-tope-awotona-poured-his-life-savings-into-calendly-now-hes-one-of-americas-wealthiest-immigrants/?sh=1a51aa3f3645.

Maheshwari, Sandeep. 2023. "Meet Shradha Sharma YourStory Founder | Episode 78" Sandeep Maheshwari. January 12, 2023. 21.54. https://youtu.be/1aS8u6LQfvc.

Mubarik, Abu. 2021. "Tope Awotona Witnessed the Murder of His Father at 12—Now He Has Built an App Valued at $3 Billion." *Business* (blog), *Face2Face Africa*. February 4, 2021. https://face2faceafrica.com/article/tope-awotona-witnessed-the-murder-of-his-father-at-12-now-he-has-built-an-app-now-valued-at-3-billion.

Pompliano, Polina. 2021. "The Profile Dossier: Tope Awotona, the Immigrant Founder Who Built a $3 Billion Software Behemoth." *The Profile* (blog). December 1, 2021. https://theprofile.substack.com/p/tope-awotona.

Sharma, Shradha. 2015. "How To Succeed As A WOMAN Entrepreneur? | Shradha Sharma | YourStory | Josh Talks" Josh Talks. August 10, 2015. 16.33. https://youtu.be/BxaYWwFtSZA.

Shen, Lucinda. 2020. "Meet the Unicorn Founder That Braved War Zones and Missed Meetings to Make His Mark on the start-up World." *Finance* (blog), *Fortune*. November 20, 2020. https://fortune.com/2020/11/19/calendly-founder-tope-awotona-startup-unicorn/.

CHAPTER 8 MAKE YOUR IDEAS STICK—START A MOVEMENT

Burt, Ronald S. 1992. *Structural Holes: The Social Structure of Competition.* Cambridge, MA: Harvard University Press.

James, Yan. 2023. "Tristan Walker, CEO of Walker and Company: The Problem with Sameness." Stanford Graduate School of Business. February 3, 2023. 51:39. https://youtu.be/NNO8tHo7EHo.

Norton, Michael L., Daniel Mochon, and Dan Ariely. 2011. "The 'Ikea Effect:' When Labor Leads to Love." *Journal of Consumer Psychology* 22, no. 3 (July): 453-460. https://doi.org/10.1016/j.jcps.2011.08.002.

Richardson, Bailey, Kevin Huynh, and Kai Elmer Sotto. 2020. "Turn Your Customers into Your Community." *Business Management* (blog), *Harvard Business Review.* January 16, 2020. https://hbr.org/2020/01/turn-your-customers-into-your-community.

CHAPTER 9 POLISH EXECUTIVE PRESENCE— NO ONE INVESTS IN YOUR IMPOSTER SYNDROME

Archambeau, Shelley. 2020. "Unapologetically Ambitious: Build the Career You Want." *IDEO U* (blog). Accessed March 10, 2023. https://www.ideou.com/blogs/inspiration/unapologetically-ambitious-build-the-career-you-want.

Blaker, Nancy M., Irene Rompa, Inge H. Dessing, Anne F. Vriend, Channah Herschberg, and Mark van Vugt. 2013. "The Height Leadership Advantage in Men and Women: Testing Evolutionary Psychology Predictions about the Perceptions of Tall Leaders." *Group Processes and Intergroup Relations* 16, no. 1 (January): 17–27. https://doi.org/10.1177/1368430212437211.

Claire, Marie. 2012. "Do You Have Executive Presence?" *Career Advice* (blog), *Marie Claire*. November 2, 2012. https://www.marieclaire.com/career-advice/tips/a7342/do-you-have-executive-presence/.

Clifford, Catherine. 2020. "'On Top of That, I Was Black and Female:' How This Silicon Valley Founder Overcame Impostor Syndrome." *Make it Black* (blog), *CNBC*. August 26, 2020. https://www.cnbc.com/2020/08/26/how-this-silicon-valley-founder-overcame-impostor-syndrome.html.

Hewlett, Sylvia Ann. 2014. "Executive Presence | Sylvia Ann Hewlett | Talks at Google." Talks at Google. June 29, 2014. 1:01:49. https://www.youtube.com/watch?v=i2QOAf-WLedE&t=104s.

Sicola, Laura. 2014. "Want to sound like a leader? Start by saying your name right | Laura Sicola | TEDxPenn." TEDx Talks. June 4, 2014. 15:32. https://youtu.be/02EJ1IdC6tE.

Young, Valerie. 2022. "Unpacking Michelle Obama's Impostor Syndrome." *Impostor Syndrome Institute* (blog). November 14, 2022. https://impostorsyndrome.com/article-featured/unpacking-michelle-obamas-impostor-syndrome/.

CHAPTER 10 ALLYSHIP IS LEADERSHIP: THE (SLOW) RISE OF DIVERSITY IN ENTREPRENEURSHIP

Aldsworth, Pamela, Katie Rae, and Alex Lykken. 2022. "Investing in inclusion: Women in the VC and start-up ecosystems." Pitchbook. Accessed 23 February 2022. https://pitchbook.com/webinars/investing-in-inclusion-women-in-the-vc-and-startup-ecosystems.

Cool, Kevin. 2022. "The only expectation I have for myself is making decisions I can be proud of." *MBA Alumni Voices* (blog), *Stanford Graduate School of Business*. July 15, 2022. https://www.gsb.stanford.edu/programs/mba/life-community/alumni/voices/tristan-walker.

Finerva. 2019. "Diversity VC Publishes Report on UK Venture Capitalists." London, UK: Finerva. https://finerva.com/report/diversity-vc-report/.

Gompers, Paul, and Silpa Kovvali. 2018. "Finally, Evidence That Diversity Improves Financial Performance." *Harvard*

Business Review, July-August 2018. https://hbr.org/2018/07/
the-other-diversity-dividend.

Kerby, Richard. 2018. "Where Did You Go to School?" *Richard
Kerby* (blog), *Medium*. July 30, 2018. https://medium.com/@
kerby/where-did-you-go-to-school-bde54d846188.

Kossinets, Gueorgi, and Duncan J. Watts. 2009. "Origins of
Homophily in an Evolving Social Network." *American
Journal of Sociology* 115, no. 2 (September): 405–50. https://
doi.org/10.1086/599247.

Pitchbook. 2021. "All In Female Founders in the US VC Ecosystem." New York City, NY: JP Morgan. Accessed March 4,
2023. https://files.pitchbook.com/website/files/pdf/2021_
All_In_Female_Founders_in_the_US_VC_Ecosystem.pdf.

Purushothaman, Deepa. 2022. *The First, the Few, the Only: How
Women of Color Can Redefine Power in Corporate Americ*a.
New York City, NY: Harper Business.

Ross, Christopher. 2014. "Reshma Saujani's Ambitious Plan
for Technology." *The Wall Street Journa*l, November 5, 2014.
https://www.wsj.com/articles/reshma-saujanis-ambi-
tious-plan-for-technology-1415237831.

Saujani, Reshma. 2014. "Reshma Saujani on Getting Girls to
Code and Why Its Good for Business." *Sponsored Content*
(blog), FastCompany. August 11, 2014. https://www.fast-
company.com/3033787/reshma-saujani-on-getting-girls-to-
code-and-why-its-good-for-business.

Somers, Meredith. 2021. "4 Ways to Be an Ally for Female Entrepreneurs." *Ideas Made to Matter* (blog), *MIT Sloan*. January 13, 2021. https://cdo.mit.edu/blog/2021/01/13/4-ways-to-be-an-ally-for-female-entrepreneurs/.

CONCLUSION

Ryder, Paul. 2001. "About That Margaret Mead Quotation." *Ohio Citizen Action* (blog). July 27, 2001. https://www.ohiocitizen.org/about_that_margaret_mead_quotation.

Shoenthal, Amy. 2022. "Women-Led Businesses Are Poised for a Comeback in 2022." *ForbesWomen* (blog), *Forbes*. January 3, 2022. https://www.forbes.com/sites/amy-schoenberger/2022/01/03/women-led-businesses-are-poised-for-a-comeback-in-2022/?sh=68e3be8965ec.

Made in United States
North Haven, CT
08 June 2023